THE
WOMAN'S
GUIDE
TO
Staying
Safe

BY CHERYL REIMOLD

THE WOMAN'S GUIDE TO STAYING SAFE

Produced by Cloverdale Press
133 Fifth Avenue
New York, New York 10003

Published by Monarch Press
A Division of Simon & Schuster, Inc.
Simon & Schuster Building
Rockefeller Center
1230 Avenue of the Americas
New York, New York 10020
MONARCH PRESS and colophon are registered
trademarks of Simon & Schuster, Inc.

Cover and book design by Robin Poosikian
Illustrations by Alphonse Tvaryanas
Typography by *Paragraphics*
Manufactured in the United States of America

1 2 3 4 5 6 7 8 9 10

Library of Congress Catalog Card Number: 84-62845
ISBN: 0-671-55620-7

Contents

FOREWORD

You are about to experience a wonderful feeling! Very soon—probably after reading the first few chapters—you will discover that you are suddenly so much more in control of your daily life, your well-being, and your safety. Just by following the sensible guidelines outlined here, you will give yourself lifelong safety insurance—a treasure no amount of premiums can buy.

In this book you will learn how to be safe on the streets, in your home, and when you travel. You'll learn how to cope with sexual harassment on the job. You'll know what to do if the worst happens—if you are raped, robbed, or attacked in any way. And you'll find out how to get help, quickly. From first aid for an accident at home to self-defense during a life-threatening attack—you will learn what to do, when, and how to do it.

As you increase your awareness of the world around you and your ability to protect yourself, you'll start feeling *free,* because awareness frees you from the fear that can paralyze you and leave you weak. And your newfound awareness will actually give you the confidence and power to face any situation squarely.

You'll find that your life is so much better when you take charge of it! And you'll enjoy life more than ever— because you won't be wasting any of it by being helplessly afraid.

INTRODUCTION

Whether you're single or married, young or old, a city dweller or a suburbanite, all it takes is a little preparation, some basic precautions, and a generous helping of common sense to be safe. This book arms you with all three. You'll learn how to prevent most dangers and you'll learn how to act sensibly and safely in any situation.

Chances are, your biggest fear is of crime; but it needn't be, because the overwhelming majority of crimes are crimes of opportunity.

What does that mean for you? It means that you can be *very safe*—if only you don't provide criminals with the opportunity to victimize you.

You can make a conscious decision *not* to be victimized, and that decision gives you a lot of power. When you are in control of your person, you send out signals that say "Go away—you're looking for trouble if you bother me." Those signals are your greatest visible form of protection.

If you've ever gone horseback riding, you know that a horse can sense the moment you land on his back *who* is master. If you're in control, he follows your signals. But if you're scared or unsure of yourself, he'll take the bit in his teeth and run away with you.

It's the same with criminals, though there ends their similarity with all noble animals! We all send out signals—

often so clear they could be in neon lights blinking around us, and criminals are tuned in to these signals. Don't forget, they want to find an easy victim who will cause them as little inconvenience as possible. So they'll pass over someone whose signals say clearly, "*I'm* in control of me! Stay away."

According to Sergeant Barbara Guarino of the Los Angeles Police Department, "Most muggers, purse snatchers, and rapists act with the opportunity. The great majority of these crimes can be prevented."

That means that, after you read this book, you will be rejected as a candidate for victimization! This is true because you are about to learn how to acquire a permanent set of safety signals that will be your first and most effective protection, wherever you go.

Staying safe is a bit like staying healthy.

First, **you learn what to avoid.**

You try not to wash your hair and then run outside on a cold day. You try to avoid drinking tap water on your first trip to Mexico.

But—say you've just washed your hair and the mailman rings the bell and your new puppy takes the opportunity to leg it for the wide open spaces. Or suppose your host in Mexico graciously offers you a drink in his home...

Then, **you take action.**

You wrap your head in a towel and put on a warm coat before dashing out into the winter streets in search of Bowser. You chase that spicy cocktail with medication prescribed by your doctor, which you packed for just such an occasion.

By the same token, you stay safe first, by knowing which situations to avoid and, second, by knowing what to do if an unavoidable situation arises.

As you read this book, you'll find that one safety device is *always* the first, the best, and the most important tool for dealing with a difficult situation: your *common sense*. We all have it, in varying degrees, but it's amazing how few people use it in an emergency—when they need it most.

This book will teach you to use your common sense to keep you safe. You'll find safety checklists and special techniques and tools to use in specific situations, study them faithfully, and try to become so familiar with them that they become simple, reflex actions you can draw on in an emergency. But what if you should find yourself in a sticky situation and you can't think clearly enough to recall exactly what to do? Just remember to trust your common sense. It can help you through any difficulty. Your common sense not only helps you out of difficult situations, it also prevents many dangerous situations from even occurring. In everything you do, let your common sense be your guide—from getting the best locks for your doors to installing a fire extinguisher in your kitchen; from avoiding deserted streets to standing back from the edge of a subway platform. This book will give you the broad base of knowledge you will need to sharpen your common sense.

1

HOME SECURITY

Your home *is* your castle—and you want to feel safe in it. Unlike a castle, though, your home is not a fortress equipped with moat and drawbridge. But that doesn't mean you can't feel protected and safe. You should and you can because all it really takes are a few precautions to become secure against intruders.

The simple fact is that one out of five burglars simply *walks* right into a house, through an unlocked door or window. In Los Angeles the police department found that in one year 60 percent of all burglaries were made with no forced entry!

So you can see that burglaries are most often crimes of opportunity. If a burglar is pretty sure he can find an unlocked door—and these studies show he has every reason to feel he can—he's not going to take on the challenge of a home that looks difficult to enter. This means that just locking your doors and windows affords you a great deal of protection.

But you can do more. Here is a simple five-step program designed to keep your home or apartment really safe. The first four steps—taking care of keys, doors, locks, and windows—are one-time precautions. The fifth—routine safety checks—is your safety-maintenance plan. And there are two more ways to give your home A-1 safety insurance: a burglar alarm and a security room.

KEYS

The easiest way to get through a door is with a key! That means burglars will go to great lengths to get your keys; it's your job to keep them out of the wrong hands.

1. Never carry identification on your key ring. If you do, and you lose your keys, you'll have issued an open invitation to the finder to ransack your home.

Here's a favorite trick of burglars who find keys with IDs on them. Someone calls your home to say he's found your keys at a store—usually the local drugstore or supermarket. He tells you they're holding the keys for you at the store. When you rush out to get them, the burglar, who's been watching your house, rushes in and cleans up.

2. Keep your house keys separate from your car keys. The best key rings are those that can be separated, with car keys on one part and house keys on the other. That way when you park the car in a garage, you can give the attendant only the part with the car keys on it.

3. Don't "hide" an extra key in a traditional place. You'd just as well leave it in the front door with a welcome note attached. Traditional places any burglar will check are under the doormat, in the mailbox, on top of the door frame, or in a nearby flowerpot.

4. If you move, have all the locks in the new house rekeyed. If you live in an apartment house, you do have to supply the landlord with a set of keys when you change the locks; but you might not want to give them to the superintendent. Even if you do trust your super implicitly, other people may gain access to his apartment and thus to your keys. On the other hand, it's comforting to know that in an emergency someone else has a set of keys.

DOORS

Since most burglars enter by the door, it's obviously the first part of your home you should secure.

1. All outside doors should be at least 1½ to 2 inches thick and should have a solid core. Doors with hollow cores or composite doors are easy to break down or bore open. If yours are hollow or composite, have them reinforced with metal housing around the edges.

2. The door should be flush with the frame. If there's space between the door and the doorframe, an intruder can wedge in a metal bar and dislodge the door. If you see a space, fasten an angle iron with carriage bolts to the top and bottom edges of the door.

3. Check the hinges. If they're on the outside, a burglar can remove the pins and pry the door open. Solution? Buy nonremovable hinge pins from a hardware store.

4. Have a viewer and a chain guard. Be sure your front door is equipped with a peephole, through which you can see people on the other side, and a chain guard. The most secure chain guard is not the one most people have on their doors. It's a heavy chain with both ends attached to a plate on the *doorframe,* not the door itself. You loop the chain around the doorknob to prevent anyone from entering.

Whatever type of chain guard you use, it should allow the door to open no more than one inch. For added protection, you can keep a rubber wedge handy to slip under the door. If an intruder tries to crash through the chain, the wedged door will make him recoil.

LOCKS

Studies show that most residential locks can be broken by an unskilled teenager in less than thirty seconds. The easiest to break is the standard spring latch. The intruder can open the door simply by pushing back the bolt (the part of the lock that connects door to frame) with a credit card, a fingernail file, or a knife.

Although good locks are expensive, remember that they cost much less than your prized possessions.

1. The best lock is a double-cylinder dead bolt.
Recent studies have shown that homes equipped with dead bolt locks are much less likely to be burglarized than others. A dead bolt lock has a bolt that can't be forced to slip back into the lock. The bolt on your lock should extend at least one inch, so that the burglar can't dislodge it by prying the door open.

The double-cylinder dead bolt requires a key for both the outside and the inside. It's safer than a single-cylinder dead bolt, which is keyed only from the outside and has a thumbscrew inside. With a single-cylinder dead bolt, if a burglar breaks some nearby glass, he can reach in and flip open the door. Keep the inside key for a double-cylinder dead bolt near the door so you can get out quickly in an emergency, but hang it somewhere out of reach of any nearby glass.

2. A good alternative is the surface-mounted rim lock. A less expensive alternative to the dead bolt is the rim lock. It's mounted on the surface of the door and has a one-inch bolt that connects with a plate on the door frame.

The best type of rim lock is the jimmy-proof rim lock. Its bolt works vertically instead of horizontally, making the connection with the plate even more secure.

3. The inside of all locks should be metal. Check with your locksmith to be sure none of your locks has a

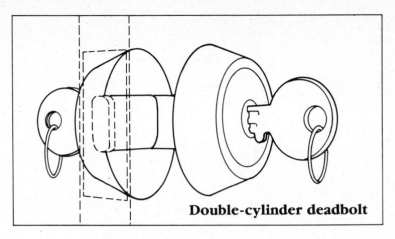

Double-cylinder deadbolt

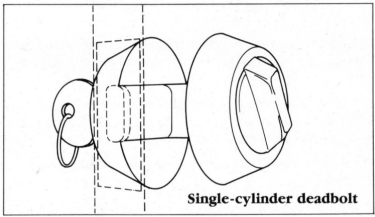

Single-cylinder deadbolt

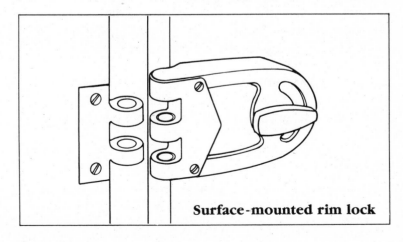

Surface-mounted rim lock

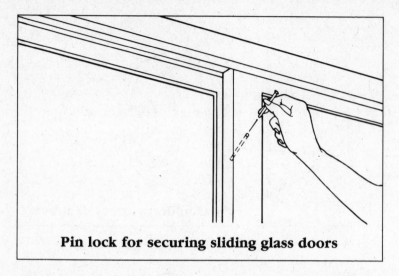

Pin lock for securing sliding glass doors

plastic interior. Plastic melts under intense heat, and in the case of a fire the lock might melt closed, preventing you from getting out.

4. Have the same key for all locks. If you get new locks, have the locksmith rekey all the locks on your doors so that you can open them all with a single key.

5. Put an extra lock on sliding glass (patio) doors. Patio doors are favorite entry points for burglars, because few people take the trouble to secure them properly. You can keep your sliding glass doors from being opened from the outside simply by cutting a broom handle or a heavy wooden pole to fit into the track. Or you can fit the door with a steel Charley Bar placed in the metal brackets between the two doors.

For extra security, you can drill a hole down through the two frames where they meet in the middle. Then you can lock them by just sticking a strong pin into the hole.

WINDOWS

Most burglars don't want to break glass because of the noise. If they can't open your windows, they'll probably go elsewhere.

1. Pin your windows. Double-hung sash windows are easy to open from the outside. The intruder simply jiggles something hard and thin between the two windows and edges the sash lock open. But—these windows are also the easiest to secure. All you have to do is drill a hole slightly downward through the inside frame and through half of the outside frame. Then insert a metal pin through the hole. The best place for the hole is the top left corner of the bottom window frame.

You can also pin your windows open for ventilation. Open the bottom window a couple of inches, then drill a hole the same way you did before and insert the pin there. Remember to close the window when you leave the house, though.

Casement windows can also be pinned. You drill a hole through the two latch sides and the handle. Then you can put your pin into the hole. This will prevent anyone from jiggling the latch loose.

Pin lock for securing double-hung sash windows

2. Secure fire-escape windows. Apartment dwellers must take extra precautions with windows leading to a fire escape. This is the burglar's favorite means of entry and quick exit. A locked metal gate is the only effective method of keeping burglars and assailants out. These days most city dwellers have gates—if you don't, you're inviting the criminal to select *your* apartment. Of course, the gate should be kept locked at all times, even when the window is open.

ROUTINE SAFETY CHECKS

Every night...

- Turn on outside lights. They should cover the front of your house and all shadowed areas. The porch light should be bright. If a bulb goes, replace it immediately. (Make sure you have some spares around!)

- Lock outside doors with a dead bolt or rim lock.

- Close all windows and insert pins.

- Draw draperies and close blinds.

- If you go to bed early, leave one inside light burning. Vary its location.

- If you have a burglar alarm system, turn it on.

Once a month...

- Check to see that air conditioners are adequately anchored.

- Check the putty securing your window panes and replace where needed.

HOME ALARM SYSTEMS

Burglar alarms are an excellent means of scaring off burglars and also of warning you of an intruder in the house. Women living alone may find an alarm system particularly comforting. These systems come with a variety of features and options, so you must shop carefully to choose the most effective one for your home. Whether you choose a complete home alarm system or a less expensive localized alarm (often more appropriate for apartments), you must consider carefully your needs and the amount of protection you desire.

Should you invest in a complete home alarm system? Only you can decide. The question is primarily financial, as complete alarm systems can run into thousands of dollars. However, the protection and peace of mind they afford may well be worth the cost, particularly if you live alone, travel a lot, have many valuables, or reside in an area where there are frequent burglaries.

If you are considering putting in a home alarm system, you should get estimates from two or three companies and explanations of the type of system they would give you. *Be sure to deal only with reputable firms.* To get the names of firms you can trust, talk or write to:

- Your insurance agent. He may recommend companies and give you information on possible home insurance deductions.

- Your local police department. They may have a list of reputable companies.

- The consumer-protection division of your local district attorney's office.

- The Security Equipment Industry Association (SEIA) or the National Burglar and Fire Alarm Association.

- Your friends who already have systems installed.

When the company representatives come to give you estimates, ask them to give you a list of their present customers. Then you can call one or two to see how the system has worked for them. You should also call the Better Business Bureau with the name of the company you're considering in order to see if any complaints have been lodged against it.

Before you get estimates, decide whether you want a system that works on contact, on movement, or with a combination of the two. The contact system consists of activated wires that set off the alarm if the burglar tries to break through them. They stop him before he enters. The movement system picks up his movements once he's in the house. Using ultrasonic waves, photoelectric devices, infrared light, or nondirectional radar, it detects motion, which interrupts its signal or wave. Its function is to call attention to the presence of an intruder inside the house. The movement alarm works only for a single area of the house. Furthermore, any movement will set it off—including your prowling house cat. And, if it's not properly adjusted, this type of alarm can activate on the slightest movement, like the natural shifting of a house's foundation, and give some people headaches.

You will probably find that a system that arms every part of every window, door, and the inside area of your house is financially prohibitive. Here you must use your common sense to help you decide how much you can afford to spend, and then see how to use it for the best protection.

For instance, you might decide to use a contact system on all the doors and windows on the main floor and basement. Then, instead of arming all the upstairs windows, you might put in an optional movement system upstairs— one with a different switch from the contact system. Then you could switch the contact system on every night, and the movement system only when everyone's out of the house.

You can also put an optional contact system on certain doors inside the house, to be activated only if you turn on a special switch. And, of course, there are many other possible combinations. Ask the companies you interview to suggest them to you and then compare the price and wisdom of each.

You should also decide whether you want an alarm that works with a key or a combination—and where you want the panic buttons (buttons that activate the alarm immediately). The best places for these buttons, by the way, are by your bed and by the front door.

When you get your estimates, compare the costs of the equipment, the installation, the monthly maintenance charge, and any service fees. Be sure that the company you choose can sell, install, and maintain the system itself and that it offers a manufacturer's guarantee against defective parts.

If you cannot afford a complete home alarm system (which can be quite expensive) or live in a small apartment, you should consider a localized alarm. There are some single, battery-operated alarms that scream if someone tries to force open the door to which they are attached. One type is fitted into a dead bolt lock. Another, less expensive variety is a device that you can place behind a door or window.

If you are in the house, these alarms will alert you to an attempted forced entry. But they have two drawbacks. One, they work only for the door or window to which they are attached. Two, if you're not at home, they may not stop a determined burglar. Police say that many burglars will wait around in hiding somewhere to see if anyone appears in response to an alarm. If neither you nor the police show up, they know all is clear and they proceed with their break-in. In an apartment, however, this type of alarm might be effective because of the close proximity of your neighbors and limited hiding places. You might also try using a single movement unit, which plugs into the wall outlet and sometimes includes optional batteries.

THE SECURITY ROOM

What if, despite all your safety precautions, someone somehow manages to break into your house? It's extremely unlikely, but it would be foolish to say it could never happen, so you should have a safe place within the home which the intruder cannot penetrate and from which you can call the police. This place is called the *security room*.

Any room in your house can be your security room, but your bedroom is probably your best choice, since that's where you'll most likely be if you hear a noise at night (the time most break-ins occur).

Here's what the security room should have:

- A thick hardwood door.

- A dead bolt lock with a key. (Leave an extra key with a trusted friend or neighbor.)

- A chain guard on the door.

- A telephone with an extension cord.

- Securely nailed windows.

- A panic button (if you have a burglar alarm system).

These are the essentials. Some experts suggest that the security room also contain:

- A light switch that controls the light in the next room

- A defensive weapon such as a baseball bat, a club, or an iron poker

Be sure your key is within easy reach—perhaps hanging on the wall near the inside of the door.

And now relax! You've made your home safe and sound.

VACATION SECURITY

There are a few extra precautions you can take to secure your home while you're on vacation. If you leave your house for an extended period, take care not to advertise the fact; but always tell a trusted neighbor and the police, so they can keep an eye on your house. Cancel all mail and newspaper deliveries or have someone pick them up for you. The same person might cut your grass as well—a shaggy lawn is a sure sign that no one is around. Also, ask your immediate neighbors to park their car in your driveway occasionally or ask their visitors to do so.

Whether or not you have an alarm system, it's a very good idea to invest in an electric timing device that will switch on various lights, radios, and televisions throughout the house at preset times. This will fool even the smartest burglar!

SAFETY CHECKS

Keys

- Never carry identification on your key chain.
- Keep house keys separate from car keys.
- Don't hide an extra key in a traditional place.
- If you move, have all locks rekeyed.

Doors

- Doors should be solid and at least 1½ to 2 inches thick.
- Doors should be flush with door frame.
- Hinges should be nonremovable.
- Doors should have a viewer and a chain guard.

Locks

- The best lock is a double-cylinder dead bolt.
- A jimmy-proof rim lock is a good alternative.
- The inside of all locks should be metal, not plastic.

- Have the same key for all locks.

- Use a wooden or steel bar to secure sliding glass doors.

Windows

- Pin them shut.

- Put a second pin hole 2 inches higher than the first, to pin windows open for ventilation.

- Use a metal gate on fire-escape windows.

Home Alarm Systems

- Consider one if you live alone, travel a lot, have many valuables, or live in an area where there are many burglaries.

- Get the names of home security system firms from your insurance agent, police department, D.A.'s office, SEIA, or the National Burglar and Fire Alarm Association.

- Check each firm's performance with customers and the Better Business Bureau.

- Be prepared with your budget, and your ideas of the kind of system best for you. Discuss them with each firm.

- Compare costs of equipment, installation, maintenance, and service. Be sure the system is guaranteed against defective parts.

Components of a Security Room

- A thick hardwood door with a dead bolt lock

- A chain guard on the door

- A telephone with an extension cord

- Securely nailed windows

- A panic button, if you have an alarm system

- A light switch controlling the next room
- A defensive weapon (bat, poker, club)

When Going on Vacation

- Tell a trustworthy neighbor and the police.
- Cancel all deliveries.
- Have someone mow the lawn.
- Ask neighbors to park cars in your driveway.
- Use electric timing devices.
- Switch on alarm.

2
PROTECTING YOUR VALUABLES

You probably already know that the safest place to store your small valuables is in a safe deposit box at the bank. There's no question that it's a nuisance to have to chug down to the bank every time you want to wear your best earrings or give a dinner party using your sterling silver. But frankly, nothing provides better security against theft, fire, and other damage than the safe deposit box.

It's also true that most of us are not so sensible that we have and use a safe deposit box. We know we should—but for convenience sake we don't. So what should we do? Here's what the experts say.

1. Make an inventory. Spend a half day one weekend going through all your belongings. List everything you own of conceivable value. Write down the serial numbers of all items that have them—television sets and other electronic equipment, cameras, typewriters, watches, cars, bicycles. Photograph your jewelry, works of art, antiques, and sterling silver. If you have art works of value, have them professionally appraised. This inventory will be necessary if you have to establish insurance or income tax claims following a robbery. It will also help you prove that an item recovered by the police is yours.

2. Store your inventory forms in your safe deposit box. Some savings and loan associations offer a safe deposit box free to clients with a certain minimum in their accounts. But however and wherever you get it, you absolutely must have that box. You should keep everything that you rarely use in it; and there's simply no other safe place for the lists, photographs, and appraisal forms that make up your inventory of valuables. If you leave your inventory papers anywhere in your home, you're just inviting the burglar who finds them to go on a treasure hunt, using your photographs and lists as clues.

3. Etch your name on your valuables with a hard-tipped electric pen. Burglars know that marked property has a lower resale value. And identifying your property will help you get it returned to you if it's recovered.

4. Store stock certificates in your safe deposit box or with your broker. A federally-sponsored insurance program offers limited protection to investors whose securities are held by brokers.

5. If you have valuables at home, hide them in hard-to-*reach* places. Repeat, that's hard-to-*reach*, not hard-to-*find*. The experts say forget about outfoxing a burglar by hiding your jewels in a place he'll never think of checking. Figure that he will check everywhere. So don't put things under the carpet, between the mattresses, in the sock or underwear drawer, in a boot, in a picture frame, in the freezer, in a teapot, in a cookie jar, or inside a curtain hem. He knows where to look and once he's found them there, he can remove them in a matter of seconds.

Instead, remember that a burglar's focus is on time—he has to work fast to get away before someone surprises him. Therefore, you want to put your things in places that would take him time to reach.

One possible place is in a hollow book on a high shelf. He'd have to go through a lot of books to find the right one. Another suggestion is behind a large chest of drawers. A third is in a home safe, either a wall safe or a safe bolted to the floor. (Smaller safes and fireproof strongboxes provide protection only against fire—not theft.)

Crime experts have different opinions about home safes. Some think that just seeing a safe may inspire a burglar to come back again to check it for valuables. Others say certain safes present too much difficulty for the average burglar to handle.

You can cover a wall safe with a picture or a hanging. As few middle-class homes have wall safes, few burglars think of looking for them. If you choose a floor safe, get one that weighs at least eight pounds and bolt it to the floor. It will be practically impossible to remove. For either type, you can install an alarm with a bell on the safe door.

6. Consider installing a security closet. The experts agree that this is the best type of home safe. You can turn any closet into a security closet by:

- Lining the floors, walls, ceiling, and door with fire-retardant or fire-resistant material

- Rehanging the door so that the hinges are inside or fitting it with nonremovable hinges

- Bracing the door frame

- Putting a dead bolt lock on the door (keep the key on your key-chain, not hidden in the house)

- Fitting the door with an alarm, connected to the central alarm system if you have one.

Then place your valuables in your security closet. One of its advantages over a safe is that it can hold large objects such as furs or home computers

Wherever you decide to store your valuables, keep it to yourself. Secrecy is one of your best forms of protection.

SAFETY CHECKS

- Make a complete inventory of your valuables.

- Store inventory list in your safe deposit box.

- Etch your name on valuables with an electric pen.

- Store stock certificates in your safe deposit box or with your broker.

- Hide valuables in the house in hard-to-reach spots.

- Consider installing a security closet.

3
KITCHEN SAFETY

The kitchen is the heart of your home—and like that vital organ, it's worth protecting, for it's also the potential source of great hazards. That one little room is literally packed with chemical, electrical, thermal, liquid, and mechanical implements designed to ease your life but with the potential to harm it. Yet you can virtually achieve 100-percent kitchen safety if you adhere to these simple safety precautions against fire, gas leaks, and accidents.

PROTECTION AGAINST FIRE

1. Keep the range clean. Don't let grease build up. After every use, clean the range with a detergent cleanser that has a surface-acting agent. If something boils over and seeps under the heating coil, sponge it up and clean the area completely as soon as the range is cool. Be careful, though. Some of these cleansers are strengthened with alkalies or other corrosive chemicals that can harm your skin or your eyes on contact. If you get any in your eye, rinse immediately and thoroughly with cold water.

2. Clean the oven at least once a week. You can cut

down on grease buildup in the oven by using foil broiling pans under your steaks and chops. But don't forget that collecting a lot of fat in a hot place is hazardous; empty them every few minutes.

3. Clean behind all major appliances and on top of cupboards and shelves at least once a year. These are prime spots for dangerous grease accumulation. Check behind the refrigerator/freezer, range if it's movable, washer/dryer, and anything else large and seemingly permanent. Of course, clean on top of them, too.

4. If you notice a frayed cord, replace it immediately. Check your old toaster, toaster-oven, blender, iron— any of those small units with frayable cords. If the cord's frayed, *don't* use the appliance until you get the cord replaced. If you decide to buy a new one, be sure it carries an Underwriters Laboratories (UL) tag.

5. To disconnect an appliance, pull it out by the plug, not the cord. That's how you cut down on frayed cords!

6. Be sure there are no curtains, paper towels, oven mitts, dishcloths, or other combustibles near the range. If a grease fire should break out, it can spread very quickly. And, always turn off the burner before you grab anything with a potholder or towel, particularly if you have a gas stove. You should also roll up your shirtsleeves so they don't come into contact with the flame.

7. If a grease fire starts in a pan, cover the pan or pour baking soda on the fire. These measures will rob the fire of the oxygen it needs to continue burning. *Never pour water on a grease fire* or carry the pan to the sink. You'll spread the flames, possibly to yourself.

8. Unplug or switch off all electrical appliances when you leave the house. Many a house fire has been started by a coffee pot that cooked dry and eventually burned. And a self-cleaning oven is definitely *on* when it's cleaning itself—to the tune of 900 degrees! Stay in the house to keep an eye on that particular electrical servant.

9. Always turn the burner off or to low when you leave the kitchen—even if it's just to answer the door or change a record. It's best to turn the stove off altogether, but if you're cooking soup or something that takes hours, it's okay to leave it on low and check periodically.

10. Install a smoke detector with an on-off switch attached. Broiling or frying foods, especially bacon, will set off the alarm, so turn it off while you're cooking and on when you're finished. Check the batteries once a month.

11. Keep a portable fire extinguisher within easy reach. An extinguisher marked A-B-C (see pp. 31–32) and weighing 2½ pounds is the best type for the kitchen.

PROTECTION AGAINST GAS LEAKS

1. Be sure the pilot flame is on. If you can't get it to come on, call the utility department immediately.

2. If you suspect a gas leak, don't stall. Call the utility company and ask for emergency service.

3. If you smell gas, hold your breath and get out of the kitchen, leaving the door open. If it's dark, *do not switch the light on*. The switch could cause a spark, which would then ignite the gas and cause an explosion. Call the fire department from a neighbor's phone. They'll call the utility company for you.

4. If you're leaving the house for an extended period, switch off the gas at the main.

PROTECTION AGAINST ACCIDENTS

1. Don't walk on slippery floors. That means don't use high-gloss waxes. And when you wash the floor, stay out of the kitchen until it's thoroughly dry.

2. Use rubber gloves when washing glasses or dishes. Dry dishes in a drying basket, not on the side of the sink. Clean up broken glass first with a wet paper towel, then with a funnel vacuum cleaner. And always resist the temptation to walk barefoot in the kitchen.

3. Don't use the wrong tools. This is probably the greatest cause of kitchen accidents. Use a can opener to open a can—not a handy knife or scissors. Use a stepstool to reach up high—not a chair, the side of a table, or a flimsy box. And don't overreach. If you can't get to what you want, ask for help or use something else!

4. Store sharp knives and other dangerous tools in a separate drawer with a child guard on it. Even if you don't have children yourself, young visitors may enter your kitchen.

5. Use chemicals with great caution. Just because they're familiar, we tend to treat some lethal poisons as safe friends. Store all cleansers in a child-proof cabinet, separate from eating or cooking wares. *Never* use one cleanser together with or right after another—the wrong combination could produce a gas that instantly kills.

6. Don't walk fast with sharp objects in your hand. And, if your kitchen has a swing door, go in carefully. You don't want to bang into someone standing on the other side who has a knife or a pair of scissors in his hand.

7. Don't touch a live electrical element (such as the heating coil in a toaster) with a metal object. To get a recalcitrant slice of toast out of the toaster, first unplug the toaster. Then you can fiddle with your fork.

8. Don't tinker. If you're not sure how to fix something, call an expert. He may overcharge, but he won't maim or kill.

9. Make sure the spring latch on your oven or broiler door works correctly. If it falls open or doesn't close correctly and the oven is on, you might burn yourself badly.

SAFETY CHECKS

To Prevent Fire

- Keep the range clean.
- Clean the oven once a week.
- Clean behind major appliances and on top of cupboards and shelves once a year.
- Replace frayed electrical cords immediately.
- Disconnect an appliance by pulling on the plug, not the cord.
- Keep all combustibles away from the range.
- If a grease fire starts, cover the pan or pour baking soda on the flames.
- Turn off all appliances if you leave the house.
- Turn off the burner if you leave the kitchen.
- Install a smoke detector with an on-off switch.
- Keep a fire extinguisher in the kitchen.

To Prevent Gas Leaks

- Be sure the pilot flame is on.

- Call the utility company if you suspect a leak.

- If you smell gas, leave the house (holding your breath) and call the fire department.

- Turn off gas at the main when you go away.

To Prevent Accidents

- Don't walk on slippery floors.

- Wear rubber gloves to wash glass and china.

- Don't use the wrong tools.

- Keep sharp objects in a child-proof drawer.

- Use and store chemicals carefully.

- Don't walk fast when carrying sharp tools.

- Don't touch a live electrical element with metal.

- Don't tinker.

- Make sure the spring latch on your oven or broiler works.

4
FIRE SAFETY

To many people, fire means panic. It shouldn't to you.

First, there are several basic precautions you can take to prevent fire. You already know what to do to keep it out of the kitchen. In this chapter you'll learn how to protect your whole house from fire.

Second, as with all safety techniques, you can learn exactly what to do if, despite your precautions, fire does break out in your house. By being prepared to escape, you *can* be safe—as you will see.

PREVENTING FIRE

In the last chapter, you learned ways to prevent fires from starting in the kitchen. Taking those precautions will substantially reduce the chance of fire in your home. However, there are dangers to be avoided in other rooms, too:

- Careless smoking—smoking in bed and then falling asleep; dropping smoldering ashes on newspapers or rugs; throwing burning matches or ashes into trash containers

- Children playing with matches and cigarette lighters

- Frayed electrical wires
- Overloaded circuits
- Faulty heating systems
- Piles of greasy rags and other combustibles

The conclusions are clear. Smoke carefully—or, better yet, don't smoke at all! Keep matches and lighters out of the reach of children. Get frayed wires repaired as soon as you notice them. If a circuit breaker switches off more than once, call your electrician immediately. Have your heater serviced once a year; and twice a year clean out all those rags and papers that have accumulated in your attic, garage, and basement.

STOPPING POTENTIAL FIRES

Smoke detectors only cost about fifteen dollars each, so there's no excuse not to own one. Most people who have installed them can tell you of at least one occasion when a detector alerted them to smoke that could have turned into a fire. This is one simple form of fire insurance you really cannot afford *not* to own. Yet only one out of four homes has it.

You should place a smoke detector near or on the ceiling in the kitchen and at the top of each stairway. You may want them in the bedrooms as well. There are two types of detectors: those with an alarm that is set off when smoke crosses a light beam and those that chemically react to smoke. Whichever type you choose, be sure it is UL approved. Battery-operated alarms are preferable, since your home's electricity can be cut off by fire. But you have to be sure to check the batteries at least once a month.

Portable fire extinguishers are another inexpensive way to save your belongings and possibly your life. You'll see four types: A, B, C, and A-B-C. Type A is for use on paper, wood, and cloth. Type B puts out fires in liquids. Type C extinguishes electrical fires. And A-B-C hits all three.

Obviously, the A-B-C type is the best, since you cannot predict which type of fire might strike. You should have an extinguisher in the kitchen, the garage, the basement, the attic if it's used for storage, and any other place where combustible substances are stored.

PREPARING TO ESCAPE FIRE

The flames don't have to reach your room to threaten your life; most deaths by fire are caused by only *three minutes* of smoke inhalation. If a fire starts anywhere in your house, you must be able to get out—fast. That means don't stop to call the fire department or root out your family photo album.

Are you sure you know the best way out of each part of your house or apartment building? Have you and your family had fire drills?

To plan your escape well, you should be aware of certain basic facts about coping with fire:

- Always sleep with the bedroom doors closed to prevent fire from spreading rapidly from room to room.

- Always *crawl* to safety; there's more oxygen near the floor.

- Touch the door before you open it. If it's hot, *do not open it.*

- Head straight for the window. Yes, the window! Keep a chain link aluminum escape-ladder in each upstairs bedroom, under the bed. Then the occupant won't have to choose between smoke inhalation and a broken neck.

Many householders buy these ladders—but few practice using them. You may not like the idea of entertaining your neighbors by scrambling out of your window like a novice cat-burglar. But if you try it, you'll realize that it's not all that easy to attach a collapsible ladder to the window and edge out of the window and down the wall. If you ever have to use the escape ladder in a fire, you'll thank your stars that you practiced it when you were calm and alert.

Escape-ladder practice is just one part of your general fire drill, which is as essential in a private house as it is in a school. And—here's the tricky part—at least one drill should be conducted at night, after the family's gone to sleep! Most of us can figure out the best exit when it's light and we're awake and alert, but it's a different matter at two o'clock in the morning.

Sit down with the other occupants of your house and plan the best escape routes from each room. Decide on a place outside where everyone will meet. Then call a fire drill at each of the following times:

- On a weekend afternoon when people are in different rooms in the house

- In the evening when they're in their rooms but not asleep

- At night when all but you are asleep

The nighttime drill will prepare people to respond correctly even when their reflexes are dulled by sleep. And, for your own safety's sake, the nighttime drill should be repeated with someone other than you directing it.

If you live in an apartment building, you should follow all the above guidelines. In the case of fire, escape through a stairway or the fire escape, but never take the elevator—it can be very dangerous! And, don't use your fire escape as an outdoor storage space or city garden; if you need to exit in the middle of the night, you might trip over something and seriously injure yourself. The key to the metal gate on the window should be close by and easy to find in the dark. During your fire drill, practice opening the gate and familiarize yourself with the workings of the fire-escape ladder.

High-rise apartment buildings are built to be virtually fireproof, so if the inside stairway is blocked wait for help in your apartment. Open the windows and call down to the fire fighters to let them know where you are. When the fire is close by or if smoke is seeping in, stuff wet towels under the front door. Replace them as needed. If the fire is in your apartment, close the door after you leave to prevent it from spreading to the rest of the building.

SAFETY CHECKS

To Prevent Fire

- Smoke carefully or not at all.

- Keep matches and lighters away from children.

- Get frayed wires repaired.

- Call electrician if circuit breaker keeps tripping.

- Have heater serviced once a year.

- Clean attic, garage, and basement twice a year.

To Stop Potential Fires

- Put smoke detectors in the kitchen and at the top of each flight of stairs.

- Put an A-B-C portable fire extinguisher in the kitchen, basement, attic, and garage.

To Escape Fire

- Plan best routes from every part of the house.

- Always sleep with bedroom doors closed.

- Crawl to safety.

- Touch door first; if hot, escape via window.

- Buy chain link aluminum ladders for each bedroom.

- In a house, practice fire drills, using ladders, in the afternoon and evening, and at night.

- In an apartment, practice fire drills, unlocking the metal window gate.

- In an apartment building, take the stairs or fire escape, *not* the elevator.

5
LIVING ALONE

As you build up your self-assurance in every area of your life—and this is what this book will help you to do —living alone becomes easier and, in fact, more fun. You discover the pleasures of decorating your home to make it a lovely place in which to live and entertain friends. Maybe some day you'll share your life and your home with another person but, right now, it can be very good to be alone.

Of course, to enjoy your home you must feel safe there—that means knowing the protective measures that keep your home inviolate. And you must be aware of the proper steps to take should danger arise.

You've already learned a great deal from the preceding chapters which you can apply to living by yourself. You know how to secure your home against intrusion (chapter 1), how to protect your valuables (chapter 2), and how to avoid fire and accidents (chapters 3 and 4). So, before you go on reading, take a moment to congratulate yourself! You have every reason to feel secure and in control.

Here are a few extra suggestions that experts on crime prevention have for women living alone. Whether you live in the country, the city, or the suburbs, these measures will protect you against unnecessary troubles.

IF YOU MOVE

How do you choose a new home or apartment? There are
certain criteria your new dwelling place should fill.

**1. The building should be secure, with solid doors,
windows, and locks.** (See chapter 1.) If it's an apartment
building, a night watchman or doorman on duty is
preferable. There at least should be an intercom between
tenants and the front door; and check to make sure it's
working.

2. Certain areas should be off limits to outsiders. In
an apartment building, the laundry, storage, and trash areas
should be open *only* to the tenants. Nobody else should be
able to enter those places—with no exceptions.

3. The garage should be close. In both a private house
and an apartment building, a garage that's part of the building itself is safer than a separate structure. You can drive
your car in, shut the garage door, and enter your house or
apartment without being out in the dark at all. If there's no
garage in the building, be sure that there is one nearby.

**4. The apartment should be on the second floor or
higher.** If you can avoid it, don't take a ground floor
apartment. They're generally the first stop for burglars and
Peeping Toms. If you do live on the first floor, the windows should have steel bars or a grille.

**5. The neighborhood should be safe, well lit, and
near shops and transportation.** A "good deal" can cost
you a lot more than you bargained for. Look critically at
the street and its surroundings. Ask around. Is the area safe?
Are the streets well lit? Is the building near a bus stop or a
train station? Is it convenient to shopping areas—and are
they well lit and populated in the evening? Be sure you are
satisfied on all these counts before you sign that lease or
deed.

WHEN YOU'RE AT HOME

1. List your initial and last name only. Check the listing of your name on your front door and mailbox. If your first name appears, remove it. Use your initial instead, and don't use *Ms., Mrs., or Miss.* Why advertise to the whole world that you're a woman living alone? If your first name appears in the phone book, call the telephone company and have it changed for next year.

2. Fool onlookers. If you're home alone in the evening, put a light or a radio on in another part of the house. It will give the impression that someone else is there. Similarly, if you answer the doorbell when you're alone in the house call out, "I'll get it, Bill!" as you approach the door.

3. Check tradespeople's I.D.'s. If they're bona fide workers, they've been trained to expect homeowners to be suspicious. They won't be surprised when you ask them to wait outside while you call the company to check their I.D.s—which is exactly what you should do. Entry under the disguise of a tradesperson is a favorite ruse of burglars and rapists. They even check to see when the gas and utility people are making the rounds in a certain area. That's when they show up at your house, in uniform, with a phony I.D. Don't trust the uniform and don't let embarrassment stop you from calling the company.

4. Don't allow anyone you don't know or aren't expecting through the front door of your apartment building. If you have an intercom system, you should always speak to the person buzzing your apartment before letting him in, even when you are expecting someone. If you don't know the person or he claims he's making a delivery you are not expecting, do not allow him entry. Would-be burglars often ring many apartments until someone foolishly lets them in—don't be that person!

5. Keep the doors locked at all times. Your first action after you walk through the door should be to turn around and lock it again. Don't leave yourself exposed; whether you're a city dweller or a suburbanite, a locked door is your best protection. .

6. Close the blinds and drapes at night. This holds true whether you live alone or not, but it's doubly important if you're by yourself. Even with the drapes shut, stay away from the window when changing your clothes.

7. Don't linger in the laundry room of your apartment building. And don't use it or any other deserted public area late at night.

8. Trim the shrubs around your windows. They make lovely hiding places.

9. If someone comes to the door for help, get the help for him or her. Never let a stranger into your home or apartment. Ask what the trouble is, then close and lock the door—leaving the porch well lit, if it's nighttime—and call the police or garage, or whatever, yourself. Make no exceptions to this rule. If the stranger tries to pressure you, lock the door and call the police immediately.

10. Set up an emergency network. Arrange with a neighbor that you will both be responsible to help the other in an emergency. You should have a code by which one of you signals the other for help in case of danger. Many people use a series of whistle blasts or flashing lights. The receiver of the message should then immediately call the police.

11. Consider a canine companion. You don't *have* to get a dog, of course, but they make great pets and marvelous protectors. A large dog may make you feel safer than a small one, although burglars have an allergy in general to barks and growls, no matter where they come from.

SAFETY CHECKS

What to Check for in a New Home

- Solid doors, windows, and locks

- Restricted laundry, storage, and trash areas

- A garage attached to or close to the building

- An apartment higher than the ground floor

- A safe, well-lit neighborhood near shops and public transportation

Safety Measures to Take at Home

- List your initial and last name only on your door, mailbox, and in the telephone book.

- Create a fake companion—using lights or a radio in another room, and calling out to someone if the bell rings.

- Check all tradespeople's I.D.s.

- Don't let anyone you don't know or aren't expecting into the apartment building.

- Keep the doors locked at all times.

- Close blinds and drapes at night.

- Don't linger in the apartment building's laundry room or use it late at night.

- Trim the shrubs near your windows.

- Don't let strangers in; make calls for them.

- Set up an emergency code with a neighbor.

- Consider getting a dog.

6
OLDER WOMEN

The good news from the U.S. Department of Justice is that older people are far less likely to be victims of any kind of crime—particularly serious violent crime—than younger people. The only possible exception is purse snatching.

These facts are comforting, but they should not be deluding. They *do* say you have no reason to spend your life in fear, but they *don't* say you can't be attacked. You still must take important precautions to protect yourself, but at the same time you can be confident in your ability to remain in control of any situation.

As always, your safety depends largely on you—how you carry yourself, whether you lock your doors and windows, and where, when, and with whom you walk and drive. Your common sense is your greatest ally. Never leave home without it (and hold onto it tightly in your house as well)!

Here are some additional tips to help you put that common sense effectively to use.

1. Be aware, alert, and careful—always. Take a moment to think over the previous day. Review what you did from morning until night. When you left the house, did you lock up carefully? Did you make sure to stay in well-lit, populated places? If you went shopping or to the bank, did you have your money ready? Did you put your wallet quickly back in your bag and keep the bag firmly clutched under your arm? In other words, did you consciously take care of yourself all day long?

In the beginning you must review each day, and after a few weeks you'll find that these safety precautions become automatic. You won't have to think about them all the time. But for now, please read over all the Safety Checks in this book and follow up on those that apply to your situation. You'll soon accumulate some simple habits that could save your life.

2. Join or start a cooperative neighborhood association. Recent studies show that very few burglaries occur in neighborhoods where people have joined together to look out for unusual or suspicious activities. Criminals, it seems, hear about the community awareness and proceed to give that community a wide berth.

This makes great sense when you reflect that most burglars tend to hit houses or apartments not too far from where they themselves live. If you've got a good neighborhood-watch program going, chances are your area has a pretty far-reaching reputation for alertness. Burglars will ply their trade somewhere else.

To start a neighborhood watch, call a meeting of the neighbors, preferably including those on the street behind you. Your group should agree to watch out for any suspicious activity on one another's property and in the neighborhood in general. Find out when people are home and assign "watch hours" to each. During each person's watch hours, he or she can go about his or her ordinary business in the house while noting any unfamiliar cars or people in the immediate vicinity. Of course, the whole group should determine to note and report any questionable activity in the neighborhood at any time.

The American Association of Retired Persons recommends that you and your neighbors also get to know each other's living patterns—work hours, regular meetings, weekend visits—and tell one another when you are going to take a trip or call in a repairman, a moving van, and so forth. This knowledge will enable all of you to spot unusual occurrences, such as a moving van arriving to clear out a house when you know no one is moving!

Events such as that are clearly noteworthy. If you see someone tearing across a neighbor's lawn with a color TV set under his arm, or if you observe a group of people detaching parts from a car—you'll know something's up. Here are some highly suspicious circumstances that your group should be prepared to note:

- Slow-moving vehicles that keep reappearing (could be looking for someone to rob or rape)

- Parked vehicles with one or two people in them (could be a lookout for a burglary in progress)

- Someone waiting in front of a house (also may be a lookout)

- Vehicle being loaded with valuables

- Abandoned cars with or without license plates (could be stolen)

- People loitering around parked cars (they may be intending to rob them)

If you see anything that worries you, don't take the law into your hands and dash over to right wrongs. Do call the police immediately. Report first *what* is going on and *where,* so they can send a car immediately, if necessary. Then give them your name, address, a description of the people or vehicle, and the license plate number if you can get it. And stay in your house until the trouble is over.

3. Stay away from junior-high and high schools at dismissal time. It's sad to say, but many purse snatches are committed by young offenders. The police have therefore advised older women to stay away from the crush of school dismissal hour (usually between 3 and 5 PM) to avoid becoming victims of this common crime.

4. Have your social security checks deposited directly into your bank account. Criminals know when Social Security checks go out. And they not only steal them from you in person but also out of your mailbox—so direct deposit definitely makes a lot of sense. With or without a Social Security Check, you should really try to avoid going to your bank on those days. It's likely to be a favored spot for purse snatchers.

If you receive any other monies that can be directly deposited into your account, arrange for that service. Your bank manager will tell you how to do it.

5. Be suspicious—please—of any offer that comes to you from a stranger or through the mail. Repeat, *any* offer. And most particularly those that present you with an opportunity to make money in your own home or receive relief for health problems without going to your doctor. The U.S. Department of Justice declares that legitimate plans of this kind are practically nonexistent.

Please carefully read the section in the Appendix of this book entitled "How to Avoid Being Conned". This is one crime for which older people *are* special targets. In addition to the advice you'll find in that section, make sure that you:

- Get medical treatment or advice only from a licensed health care practitioner. That includes sight and hearing checkups, as well as glasses and hearing aids!

- Never send for a medical diagnosis, laboratory test, cure, or "miracle drug." You'll lose your money and possibly your health.

- Throw away any offers of retirement real estate at incredibly low prices. Such offers are indeed unbelievable.

If you're unsure at all about any transaction you're considering, don't hesitate to call one of the following agencies. Remember, their reason for existence is to serve you. Use them.

- The Better Business Bureau
- Your city's hearing and speech center
- The Heart of America Eye Center
- The Social Security office
- Your senior citizens center

SAFETY CHECKS

- Be aware, alert, and careful.
- Join or start a neighborhood-watch association.
- Stay away from schools at dismissal time.
- Have your Social Security checks deposited directly into your bank account.
- Be suspicious of any mail offer, especially those that promise you ways to make money at home or to take care of your health without going to a regular doctor.

7

SURVIVING "ACTS OF GOD"

Most insurance companies will tell you that you can't insure against what they call "Acts of God"—floods, hurricanes, and other natural disasters. Well, you may not be able to get financial coverage, but you certainly can prepare for them to ensure that you suffer the least damage possible.

Experts say that if disaster hits, knowing what to do is 90 percent of the battle. Therefore, you should take the following precautions:

1. Make a list of all possible emergencies and what to do if they occur. Involve everyone living in your house in this written plan. Then make copies of it and place them in plastic covers in drawers near every phone in the house. The list should include:

- Where each person should go in case of natural disaster

- What everyone should do if public transportation is not working

- Whom to call in a crisis: phone numbers of relatives, neighbors, and friends who will help

- Emergency numbers: fire, police, ambulance, doctor

2. Learn the location of your nearest hospital emergency room. Take the time to actually drive there to find the quickest route from your house and to locate the parking lot and the emergency entrance. You may save some truly critical moments in an emergency.

3. Carry your insurance card with you. If you're on someone else's policy, note the name of the insurance carrier and the policy number.

4. Keep a set of blackout or brownout tools in working order. This includes: two flashlights, a battery radio, a supply of firewood if you have a fireplace, and three or four kerosene lamps.

The firewood will keep you and the house warm in the case of an extended blackout. Besides providing light, the kerosene lamps will also give the house a little extra warmth and so consequently prevent pipes from bursting. Be sure you follow instructions for lighting the lamps; if they're not running well, they can give off carbon monoxide gas. Put them out if you smell gas or a charred odor or if they're flickering and sputtering.

5. During a blackout or brownout, close the windows, lock all doors, and stay inside. This is the criminal's favorite time—when houses are dark and the police are busy keeping basic services functioning.

6. Have a lightning rod installed on your house. But be sure it's installed by an expert who knows how to ground it properly. If it's not well grounded, the rod will *attract* lightning instead of deflecting it.

7. If you live in an area known for hurricanes or tornados, keep a set of emergency supplies. Thanks to modern technology, we usually hear of these conditions in time to leave the area before the storm arrives. However, it's not always possible to pick up and leave. You should have handy: a battery radio, two flashlights, canned food, and bottled drinking water. If you don't have time to evacuate, open the windows on the side of the house away from the approaching storm, and take shelter in the basement.

8. If dangerous gale winds strike, seek shelter. If you have a basement, go there immediately. If not, get to the innermost part of your house or apartment. To stay out of danger from falling materials, hide under a heavy piece of furniture. One or two windows should be slightly open so that the air pressure in the house equals that outside.

9. Don't leave the house in an earthquake. During an earthquake, the safest places to be are under a doorway or a strong, heavy table. Take care to stay away from windows, mirrors and, of course, falling objects. If you're caught outside you should head as quickly as possible to the nearest open space. Look out for power poles and debris from tall buildings.

SAFETY CHECKS

- Keep an emergency list by each telephone.

- Find your nearest hospital emergency room.

- Carry health insurance information with you.

- Keep a blackout or brownout kit in the house.

- In a blackout or brownout, lock up and stay inside.

- Have a lightning rod installed.

- Keep a storm emergency kit.

- In a dangerous storm, go to the basement or an inside room and get under a piece of furniture.

- In an earthquake, get under a heavy table or doorway; if outside, seek an open space.

8
SEXUAL ADVANCES IN THE OFFICE

When women encounter sexual advances made in the office, their first reaction is usually fear. Not fear for their safety, but fear for their jobs. A lascivious boss can indicate clearly that you can look elsewhere for work if you reject his advances. It's very easy for an outsider to say, "Tell him he can keep his job." It's not so easy to know what to do when you enjoy your job or when you need that job to put food on the table. Besides, no woman should be forced to leave her job because of the wrongful conduct of another person.

Your very best weapon against sexual harassment on the job—or anywhere else, for that matter—is the image you project of yourself. That doesn't mean that if you are harassed it's in any way your fault, but the way you perceive and carry yourself can influence people's image of you. Remember, nobody likes to be rejected. When a man makes sexual advances to a woman, he usually thinks he has a good chance of success. If you show very clearly that you are a serious professional who is not interested in office play, you will probably forestall most advances.

This does not mean you have to dress like a nun or try

to look like a tank. It does mean that you can set up bar-
riers to sexual advances before they begin, just by the way
you look and act. Here are some guidelines:

- Dress to look attractive, not sexy.

- Talk to men in exactly the same way you talk to women
  in the office—with no unspoken, suggestive messages.

- Unless everyone in your company uses first names, keep
  a certain distance in conversations by calling people Mr.
  ———.

- When people around you are talking with sexual innuendoes, walk away.

- Don't regularly encourage or accept invitations to one-
  on-one lunches or dinners.

- Don't be playful, teasing, flirtatious, or "cute." You'll
  attract exactly the kind of attention you want to avoid.

Altogether, your personal attitude and body language
should say, "We are all mature, respectable people working
together. Let's not lose our self-respect *or* our respect for
each other."

Most overt sexual advances are preceded by some
unspoken signals between the two people. No guidebook
could list them all for you, but you know one when it
appears. It's a look, a gesture, even a raised eyebrow that
says, "We may be talking about your contributions to the
marketing effort, but what I'm really thinking about is sex
with you."

If you receive such signals and don't immediately
parry them with a clear NOT INTERESTED sign, the unspoken
suggestion may well turn into open advances or
harassment.

How do you show you're not interested? It is important to signal clearly that you have got the message and that

your answer is *no*. Breaking eye contact might be misinterpreted as a coy or bashful response. It's better to sit up or stand straight and look directly at the other person with an expression that says, "I respect you as I respect myself. I am not available for sex. Please don't do or say anything that would make me lose my respect for you."

But what if the man persists, despite your clear signals? What if he makes it clear that keeping your job or getting your promotion depends on going to bed with him?

Here's a good psychological approach to start with. It is the least disruptive and usually the most enduring solution. People tend to behave the way they are treated. See the good in someone, and he'll often start feeling and behaving like a good person. See the creep—and you're likely to inspire creepy actions! So, try to see the decent, kind human being inside that person who is at the moment being propelled by an overwhelming sex drive. But you must really see the good person first. The technique won't work if you just try to fake it.

Once you've caught a glimmer of decency, speak to it. Talk to your boss in a calm, friendly tone. Tell him how much you enjoy your job. Say that it has been a pleasure to work for someone you can respect and from whom you can learn. Then look clearly into his eyes and say, "I like you and I like working for you. But I can't accept your proposal. Can we go on working together as two professionals with mutual respect?"

Now, you have put the ball in his court. You haven't offended or rejected him or put him down in any way; you've merely made clear your conditions for working. And you've shifted the roles from *powerful boss and helpless employee* to *two professionals who like and respect each other.* The technique usually works very well.

If this approach doesn't stop him, you can go straight to personnel and report your boss's behavior to them. Unfortunately, if there are no witnesses, it's your word against his. Although it might be easier to avoid any further unpleasantness by asking straight off for a departmental transfer, if you want to keep your present job, there are some constructive measures you can take. If the personnel department indicates that they won't do anything to help without proof of harassment—get it for them. Build up a file of evidence of your boss's sexual advances, and then present it to the director of personnel and possibly the president of the company. Here are some ways to do it:

- Make detailed notes of his propositions to you. Write down what was said and when.

- Ask other women in the company if they have been sub-jected to the same harassment. If so, see if they are will-ing to go on record about it.

- Get a friend to listen when you're next alone with him.

- Ask a friend or a member of a local women's support group to come to your house. Then call your boss on the phone about a business matter and have her listen in on the conversation. If he makes the usual suggestions, you'll have a witness.

For simplicity's sake, I've called the male aggressor your boss. The same advice applies to advances made by a co- worker or a client.

If you have built up evidence against someone, it's a good idea to contact your local women's support group for job equity. They will send you someone experienced who can help you present your case effectively. You can find your local support group listed under "Guide to Human Services" in the blue pages of your phone book. If you can't find an organization specifically devoted to issues of job equality, call another women's help group, tell them of your problem, and ask for the name of an organization that can help you.

SAFETY CHECKS

To Prevent Harassment in the Office

- Don't wear suggestive clothing.

- Talk to men in the same way you talk to women.

- Use Mr. ——— rather than first names (unless everyone in your office goes by their first names).

- If the talk around you takes on sexual innuendoes, walk away.

- Don't accept too many private lunch or dinner invitations.

- Don't flirt.

If You Are Harassed

- Show the other person that you see him as a decent human being with whom you want a working relationship built on mutual respect.

- If he persists, see the personnel director. Describe what happened or request a departmental transfer.

- If you want to stay where you are and personnel won't step in without evidence, get it by
  - Noting the time and place of all his advances
  - Asking other women if he has bothered them, too
  - Getting a friend to listen when he is with you
  - Calling him with a friend listening in to witness the conversation.

- Call your local women's support group for job equity to get help in presenting your complaint.

9
TRAVELING SOLO

Traveling alone can be an exciting, interesting, and enriching adventure—or a nightmare. It all depends on how well you prepare, and I'm not just talking about packing.

Many women are simply not used to traveling alone. They don't have much experience with all the details that it entails: taking care of plane tickets, figuring out the tip on cab fare, checking in and out of hotels, coping with luggage. One woman on her first business trip admitted she was so nervous about making her plane connections that she had no time to worry about staying alone in a big- city hotel room!

The trouble is that woman had every reason to worry about staying alone in a hotel. Her nervousness and preoccupation over her plane connection would show in her expression and behavior—and would probably make her careless about more important precautions. She would look assailable.

But there's no reason your solo travels can't be safe and thoroughly enjoyable; all it takes is careful preparation for every phase of the trip. Knowing that you are in control will give you the air of confidence that keeps trouble-makers away. As always, self-assurance and alertness are your two greatest allies. These qualities are actually like watchdogs! You can see why.

Imagine one woman waiting agitatedly in line at the airline ticket counter...stepping from one foot to the other...constantly checking in her handbag (and periodically dropping something out of it)...kicking her overfull, overlarge suitcase along with her (and stopping periodically to refasten the catch)...and all the time glancing nervously at her watch.

Now imagine another woman standing composedly in another line. Her ticket is ready in her hand, her slim bag is attached to the traveling wheels beside her, and her eyes keep a calm watch on the goings-on around her.

Which one do you think a thief or rapist would choose?

In this chapter, you will learn how to manage every phase of your travel, from dealing with airline tickets to securing your safety in a hotel room. The suggestions you will find here come from experts in crime prevention and from women who have done extensive traveling on their own. Next time you go, you'll be able to "sit back, relax, and enjoy your trip," as they say on the airlines, knowing *you* are in control of it.

BEFORE YOU LEAVE

1. Type up an itinerary for yourself and leave a copy with a relative or friend. For each day you'll be away, your itinerary should list: the city, the hotel (full name—there may be more than one branch in a big city), the hotel's telephone number, your arrival and departure dates, and your reservation confirmation number, if you have one.

This itinerary serves three purposes.

One, it means someone will always know where you're supposed to be and where to reach you if necessary.

Believe me, it's very comforting to feel that someone knows where you are when you're out there all alone!

Two, you will have important information at your fingertips when you need it. If you're going to two or three different places, it's very easy to mix up the hotels. You could get into a taxi at the airport and ask the driver to take you to the Sheraton, when in fact you're registered at the Hilton. This wouldn't be a sudden case of amnesia and it certainly wouldn't be unusual. If you stayed in a Sheraton in Boston on Monday night, a Hilton in Chicago on Wednesday, and a Sheraton in Cleveland the week before, it's not surprising if you mix up your Sheratons and Hiltons in New York on Friday! With your itinerary in hand, you won't make mistakes like this—mistakes that leave you temporarily baffled and upset and, therefore, not in control.

Three, your confirmation number will help you straighten things out if the hotel informs you that they do not have your reservation.

2. Don't take more than $400 in cash. That's the limit experts recommend. If you need more, use traveler's checks or credit cards. And don't put all your cash in your wallet, either. Keep up to $50 in your wallet for immediate use and store the rest in your purse where it won't be seen when you pull out your wallet to pay for your coffee.

3. Put your credit cards, tickets, stored cash, travelers checks, and pocket calculator in a safe place— and keep them there. If you put them in a zippered pocket of your handbag, that's where they should stay for the entire trip. Then you won't have to go crazy rummaging through all your things at the reservation desk or ticket counter. Remember, anything that takes away your control of yourself or your belongings is an absolute no-no.

4. Pack as little as possible and when possible only

take a carry-on bag. You want to be independent and free to move at will, so don't put yourself in the position of being unable to carry your own luggage. The man who offers to help you with your bags may be planning to help himself to you. Or, he may take off with your possessions before you know what's happened. It's one of the oldest tricks there is.

Today's lightweight luggage is perfectly manageable, especially if you buy a set of portable wheels to save your arms and shoulders on those long walks through the airports. And you can hang a garment bag on the rack provided in the plane.

Aside from the convenience, there are some practical reasons why you may not want to place your luggage in the hold. If you land at the airport late at night and your bag is one of the last to arrive—well, waiting around by yourself in a deserted luggage claims area is not a good idea. And if your bag is one of the first to be unloaded and you haven't arrived at the luggage claim area yet, someone else may pick it up and dash away with it before you even arrive. It's happened many times before.

AT THE AIRPORT

1. Keep your belongings close to you at all times.
Airport thefts of suitcases are booming. Have all your cases right next to you when you check in, and try to keep a hand or arm over them when you sit down to wait. Don't leave them by your chair when you get up to check the departure time or grab a drink of water. And don't leave anything outside the cubicle in the ladies' room.

You can see why it's worth the effort to travel light! Sometimes, however, it's necessary to take a lot of bags or parcels along. If so, store your bags in one of the coin-operated lockers near the departure gate. Then you'll be free to move around while you're waiting, and your luggage will be safe and close by when you have to board.

2. Hold on to your ticket. Don't stuff it into your coat pocket or the open side pocket of your handbag. Unused tickets are redeemable for cash, as all thieves know. Some enterprising robbers have even formed businesses that steal and resell valid tickets. Also, never show your ticket to anyone other than a uniformed airline employee. If someone else asks to see your ticket while you're waiting for the plane, refuse. Ticket thieves have a trick of taking a passenger's valid ticket (which they soon sell or use themselves) and, in exchange, giving the passenger a useless boarding pass taken out of a trash container.

3. In the cocktail lounge, read. There's no reason why you shouldn't wait for your plane in the cocktail lounge, but, again, let your common sense be your guide. A single woman sitting at the bar, gazing around and tossing back several stiff Scotches to ward off fear of flying may end up with some unpleasant troubles on the ground. So sit at a table, not at the bar, look relaxed and in charge, and open your book or newspaper. You'll look unapproachable. In the cocktail lounge, as anywhere else, never flash a wad of bills.

4. Ask directions from airline personnel only. Airports can be confusing, and they have many tortuous, deserted pathways. Don't rely on those cryptic signs or your own sense of direction. Ask an airline official how to get to the gate, ladies' room, or wherever you want to go.

ON THE PLANE

1. Take charge of your belongings yourself. Don't give the impression of being a breathless, helpless female. If your carry-on luggage is really too cumbersome or heavy to toss on to the overhead rack, ask the flight attendant for help. If a passenger offers to help and you're holding up the people waiting to board, accept his offer and thank him graciously, but don't get involved in a lot of follow-up conversation. Another reason for traveling light!

2. Keep your handbag close beside you if you sleep. And, of course, always carry it with you when you leave your seat.

3. If someone bothers you, tell the flight attendant. Flight attendants are trained to deal with such problems. Don't be afraid to ask for help. You don't want the person to continue bothering you on the ground.

4. Don't give out the name of your hotel. If you're engaged in a friendly conversation with a fellow passenger, and he casually asks you which hotel you're staying at, say, "Actually, I'm staying with a friend who moved out here."

FROM THE AIRPORT TO THE HOTEL

1. Take an airport limo, a bus, or a taxi to your hotel. Don't join a group taxi with people you don't know. It may be hard to believe, but this is another favorite ploy of criminals. They dress respectably, arrange for a group taxi with bona fide passengers, and then hold up the whole carload, driver included.

2. Compare the taxi driver's face with his photograph before you close the door. If the face and photo don't match, get right out of the cab. Say, "Oh, my goodness, I've left one of my bags in the airport." Then grab your luggage and start back to the terminal. If you can, get his license number and tell an airport official or call the police.

3. Figure on about $25 for a cab ride (including tip) from the airport to the center of any major city. And then sit back and feel relaxed and competent in the cab.

Don't sit on the edge of your seat, watching the meter and wildly trying to tote up the probable tip as you go along. You will look inexperienced and vulnerable. Instead, wait until you arrive at the hotel, then look at the meter and calmly add 15 percent. Take your time; don't get into a flap. You're not expected to be a mathematical whiz.

AT THE HOTEL

1. Register using your initial and your last name. And don't add "Ms." or "Mrs." You don't want to advertise to everyone who sees the registration records that you're a woman alone.

2. Don't mention your room number when you get your key. To protect you from unwanted "visitors," some hotels now give out keys with numbers that differ from the number of your room. Only two people should know your room number—you and the desk clerk.

3. Be sure you know your room number. If you stayed in another hotel the night before, you might very easily mix up your present room number with the one from the night before—especially if the numbers are similar. It happens to people all the time. But the results can be unpleasant for a single women if she starts fiddling with the doorknob of a strange man's room.

4. Check to see if anyone follows you when you leave the registration area. If you suspect someone, turn around and go back. Go to a house phone in the lobby and pretend to be dialing. If the person was following you, he'll be put off by the notion that you're calling someone in the hotel to come and meet you. Watch out of the corner of your eye until the suspect disappears.

If, despite your precautions, someone does follow you to your room, walk past the door and down the hall, and then turn around and go back to the elevator. He won't like your passing him. Or, knock on the door of your room as if someone were already inside. If he's still hanging around, head for the nearest house phone and call the front desk for help.

5. If you do not have a key and a porter carries your bags to your room, wait five minutes before you leave the lobby. You do not want to be caught standing around alone in an upstairs hotel corridor. Let the porter arrive at your door before you.

If your key for some reason won't fit the lock, do not let the porter leave you alone in the corridor while he goes down to get another key. Go with him.

6. Double-lock and chain your door as soon as the porter leaves. For added protection, you can buy a small travel lock that slides between the door and its frame.

7. If there's a knock on your door—don't open it. If you've ordered room service, look first through the peep-hole to see if your caller is indeed a uniformed waiter with a tray. If you're not expecting anyone and you don't know the person outside, don't open the door.

8. When you leave your room, leave at least one light on. This makes it much more difficult for anyone to sneak in and hide. If, on your return, you open the door to a darkened room, close it again immediately and get back to the lobby, and, of course, tell the people at the front desk.

As an added precaution, whenever you return check potential hiding places in your room. Leave the door open—with a chair there to keep it open, if necessary— and look under the bed, in the closets, behind the drapes, and behind the shower curtain. If you should uncover someone, yell "FIRE!!" at the top of your lungs. You'll bring the whole floor out to your aid.

IN THE ELEVATOR

1. Don't get on if there's a single man inside. If you're upstairs, just wait. You could easily be waiting for an elevator going in the other direction. If you're in the lobby, you can start to enter, then say, "Whoops, my keys!" and head back to the lobby.

2. Stand near the alarm bell and floor buttons. If you're verbally or physically accosted, scream and push the alarm and the next floor button.

3. If someone unsavory-looking gets on and you're alone—push the button of the next floor and get off. If you're standing near the button panel, as you should be, you can do it before he even sees you.

4. Ask at the front desk if the hotel has a "return to room" escort service. Many of the larger hotels in big cities have instituted this service for women.

EATING ALONE

You can always call room service. After a busy day's work, it might be nice to relax in your room in a comfortable robe with a good spy thriller and a club sandwich by your side.

　　If you want to dine in a restaurant, use the one in the hotel and take your thriller along for company. Follow the normal precautions of keeping alert, hiding your cash, and holding your purse in your lap. If you look aware and in control, it's most unlikely that anyone will try to bother you. Call the manager if someone does approach you. If he follows you out, go to the front desk and ask for help.

　　Remember, when you're traveling alone you've always got a source of help available for any sticky situations. Your *common sense!* Keep it well sharpened, and enjoy your trip.

SAFETY CHECKS

Before You Leave

- Type an itinerary and leave one with a friend.
- Don't carry any more than $400 in cash, keeping only $50 in your wallet.
- Keep credit cards, tickets, travelers' checks, stored cash, and pocket calculator in a safe place, and don't put them anywhere else.
- Travel light with carry-on luggage.

At the Airport

- Hold on to your bags.
- Hold on to your tickets.
- In a cocktail lounge, read, and don't flash cash.
- Ask directions from airline personnel only.

On the Plane

- Take charge of your own belongings.
- Keep your purse beside you if you sleep.
- If someone bothers you, tell the flight attendant.
- Don't tell other passengers where you're staying.

From the Airport to the Hotel

- Take an airport limo, bus, or taxi—not a "group taxi."
- Check the cab driver's face against his photo.
- Figure on $25 fare to a midtown hotel.

At the Hotel

- Register with your initial and last name only.

- Don't repeat your room number out loud.

- Be sure you know the number before you go to your room.

- Check to see if you're being followed. If you are, go to a hotel phone. If he persists, tell the people at the front desk.

- Let the porter leave with your bags a few minutes before you go up to your room.

- Always double-lock and chain your door.

- Don't open the door to anyone without first looking through the peephole. And then, only open to an expected caller.

- Leave a light on in your room when you leave and check for intruders—with the door open—when you return to your room.

In the Elevator

- Don't get on with a lone man.

- Stand near the alarm bell and floor buttons. Use one or the other if someone disturbs you.

- Get off at the next floor if a suspicious-looking character enters.

- Ask if the hotel has a "return to room" escort service.

Eating Alone

- Use room service or the hotel restaurant.

- Stay aware and in control.

- Tell the manager or the people at the front desk if anyone bothers you.

THE BIG WORLD
PART 3

10
CITY STREETS

Nobody wants to be a victim—nobody asks to be a victim—but few people take the time to consciously avoid victimization. Although most women exercise some sort of common sense, every woman needs to take the time to review her most effective means of self defense. In this chapter, you'll learn the "street smarts" that signal to the criminal, "Don't bother me. I can take care of myself."

Experts in victimology have identified the following preventive steps you can take to avoid becoming a victim of street crime. You should avoid:

1. Being alone. No criminal wants to be identified or possibly attacked by someone else. Try to find someone to walk with, or attach yourself to a crowd of people heading in your direction. Many women ask around in their offices to see who lives near them. Then they can arrange to go to and from work together.

This may sound ridiculous, but it's worth the trouble. Consider the following study by Community United Against Violence, in San Francisco: They found that if you walk with one other person, you reduce your risk of assault by 67 percent; if you have two or more companions, your risk is 90 percent less than walking by yourself.

2. Being out late. The chances of attack are three times greater during the night than during the day, and in fact most street crime takes place at 11 P.M. Furthermore, street criminals know that paydays are usually the first or the fifteenth of the month, or a Thursday or Friday. If you're out on those nights, do yourself a favor and take extra precautions.

3. Deserted side streets. This applies to residential as well as downtown areas. Remember, like the spider and the fly, the criminal wants his victim where he can have her all to himself. His parlor is the dark, empty street. Don't walk into it.

4. Large parks or parking lots. These areas are hard to patrol and easy to hide in. Park your car on a fairly busy street or in an open-air lot with plenty of people around. And walk around the park (on the sidewalk *across* the street from the park), not through it.

5. Being dressed unusually. On the street, particularly at night, your goal should be to blend in, not stand out. This is one place where you don't want to attract attention. The street-smart woman saves high fashion and startling effects for indoors. Remember, super-high heels and tight skirts impede movement—and the guy lurking in the dark doorway knows that. It's an extra bother, but it's worth carrying your spike heels and wearing flats if you have to walk to the party. Throw a plain coat over your slinky red dress and dazzling diamonds—even if they're fake!

6. Carrying lots of packages. They not only weigh you down and make you look like an easy prey, but they may also look worth stealing.

7. Walking near cars parked along the road, thick trees or bushes, darkened alleys or doorways. Or anywhere else your common sense tells you is a good hiding place for someone who's up to no good.

8. Taking shortcuts. When you find yourself thinking, "Oh, I can take a shortcut along X Street," it's a good bet that X Street is either a dark alley or a sparsely travelled road. The reason is obvious: If X were the normal way to go, you'd use it regularly. It's a "shortcut" because it's not the regular way—the way most people go. Make life simple for yourself and decide now that you will not take shortcuts, ever. (You wouldn't take a shortcut across the marine museum via the sharks' tank, would you? Even if it did offer the shortest distance between two points.)

If you follow these Eight Steps of Prevention, you will considerably lessen your chances of being involved in a street crime. Remember, a street criminal doesn't want to be caught. His allies are darkness and emptiness; his prey, someone who looks easy to grab and subdue, and who looks worth the trouble.

Your allies are well-lighted, populated places. And, for perhaps the only occasion in your life—you want to look extremely uninteresting.

You've taken the Eight Steps of Prevention—and now you are out on the street. You still want to be in control, should a difficult situation arise. Now is the time to move from avoidance to action.

Again from the experts, here are Eight Effective Actions you can take to prevent victimization on the streets. This is your *active* set of street smarts.

1. Feel confident and in control. Remember that horse in the Introduction! You can take control simply by feeling confident. Criminals are scared, frantic, insecure people who somehow got warped during their lifetime and usually don't seek challenges. If you really believe that you are in control, they'll pick up this feeling when they look at you. And they'll look elsewhere, for an easier prey.

Experts have found that it takes a mugger only seven

seconds to size up a victim. Communications expert Betty Grayson videotaped 100 pedestrians for seven seconds each. When she showed the tapes to prisoners at Rahway State Prison in New Jersey, they consistently picked out the confused or unsure ones as "more muggable." The lesson? We can determine our own safety, first of all by feeling in control.

2. Walk purposefully, with body straight and head erect. The "muggable pedestrians" that the prisoners picked out were generally perceived as slow or clumsy. Other studies show that street criminals are drawn to people who appear to be distracted, lost, or "in the clouds." Enjoy your walk; but keep your feet firmly on the ground. If you're lost in a strange city, try to *look* as if you know where you're going. Then head for a respectable store or restaurant and ask for directions. And then take a bus or a cab.

3. Be alert and aware of your surroundings. If a person or a group approaching you looks suspicious, move away. Cross the street...hail a cab. Trust your intuitions. Street smarts sometimes clash with polite social conventions. If someone stops to ask you for directions or a cigarette and you feel uneasy, keep on walking. You can make up for it later with a special act of courtesy to a friend or spouse!

4. Hold your purse close to your body. The experts advise not carrying a purse at all, but most women find this unfeasible. Grip your purse firmly under your arm or in your hand, to draw it away from the eye and the hand of the greedy beholder, and carry it on the side away from the street so passing cyclists can't grab it.

Do not wrap purse straps around your neck or your wrist; if someone does make a grab for your bag, you could be seriously injured. If you really need only your wallet and your keys with you, slip them into an inside pocket and leave your purse at home.

And what about the wallet and the keys? A little subterfuge can protect these. It's a very good idea to keep an old wallet in a prominent place—your coat pocket or right inside your purse. This wallet shoud contain $10 to $20, some old identification (not your present address), and old photos. If someone does accost you, give him this wallet. It has enough money in it to keep him from committing an act of aggressive frustration, but it doesn't have your address or credit cards. Keep your other money, credit cards, and identification elsewhere.

Now, the next point is going to sound like a nuisance, but you'll quickly see its wisdom. You should not keep your keys in your purse. If someone does manage to make off with your purse, you don't want them to have the keys to your home as well—particularly if your license or other forms of identification were in your handbag. Even if they don't break into your home, you still must change your locks. Start keeping your keys in your pocket. Like any other habit, it will soon become the natural thing to do.

5. Note safety landmarks. On your regular routes to and from work or friends' houses, note the places you can go to for help in an emergency. These include:

- Police stations

- Fire stations

- Police call boxes

- Public telephones

- Stores or businesses that remain open late

- Buildings with doormen

You probably won't ever have to use any of them—just as you probably won't have to use the portable fire extin-

guishers you've placed at strategic points in your home.
(What? You don't have portable fire extinguishers?? Read
chapter 4!) But being street wise means taking precautions
—and then being able to relax and enjoy life, knowing *you*
are in charge. After all, that's what this book is really all
about—putting you in charge of your life.

So note your landmarks and don't hesitate to use them
if your intuition tells you something's rotten in the immediate vicinity.

**6. Have your keys ready when you're approaching
your home or car.** Don't pause somewhere to root
around in your purse for them because you can't be alert
while fumbling in your bag. Besides, it's not a good idea to
stand in public places with your purse open. You show
passers-by your belongings and—if purse snatching happens to be their weakness—you actually invite them to
indulge themselves, at your expense. It's like opening a bag
of gold-wrapped Godiva miniatures in front of a confirmed
chocoholic. For the same reasons, don't carry a purse that
doesn't zip or snap shut—and always keep it closed!

7. Walk against the flow of traffic. Then no one can
drive up behind you without your seeing him. If you forget
to do this and a man in a car does threaten you, scream
and run in the opposite direction. He'll have to turn the car
around to pursue you—which he probably won't do. Even
if he does, you've bought yourself the time to run to safety
or get help.

But—it's much easier to go against the flow!

**8. If you're being followed, look, move, and attract
attention.** Your first act if you think you're being followed
is to look behind you and see who's there. It sounds
obvious, but many women do just the opposite. Some misguided instinct tells them that if they don't look, the follower will fade away, and if they do, he'll take it as an

invitation.

It doesn't work that way. If someone is intentionally following you, he's not going to change his mind because you don't seem to notice him. On the contrary, he doesn't want you to notice him until he's close enough to grab you.

So—look firmly behind you. No one can mistake a clear, critical look for a come-on. Your pursuer may very well give up the chase when he sees you're alert, aware, and capable.

Then cross the street and go on walking. See if he's still there. If he is, your goal is to stay away from him and attract attention.

There are several ways to do this. Choose the one that fits the time and place and that you can do with a minimum of hesitation. Here are your options:

- Go up to a stranger on the street and ask if you can stay near him or her until help comes or until you can get a cab. Explain the situation, pointing out the suspect. He may fade away, but he could be hiding so try not to continue your walk alone.

- Go into an open business, restaurant, store, or gas station. Call a friend or the police to come and pick you up.

- If there's one nearby, go to a police call box or dial the emergency number from a pay phone. You should find out now whether or not your community has this emergency number; not all do. Your local police department can tell you. If your community does not have one, dial "0" and say, "Emergency—Police!" The operator will connect you directly.

- If there's no help around, and no lighted building, stay in the middle of the sidewalk. If you're near some parked cars, check to see if you can find an unlocked one. Then get into the car and lock the doors. (Don't worry if you set off the car alarm; you *want* to attract attention.) Honk the horn repeatedly until someone comes. Don't just keep the horn down; people may think it's stuck and may not come to investigate.

- If you're in a residential area, run to a house with lights on and knock loudly on the door. The occupants may not let you in, but they will probably be willing to call the police for you. Ask them to leave the light on outside the door if you have to stay there.

Congratulations! You have now developed a good repertoire of street smarts. Don't be content with a single reading, though. You want to turn these simple safety measures into reflex actions. For the next few days, run through the following checklists before you go out. Then relax and enjoy the wonderful feeling of being in control of your life.

SAFETY CHECKS

Eight Steps of Prevention

Avoid:

- Being alone.

- Being out late.

- Deserted side streets.

- Large parks or parking lots.

- Being dressed unusually.

- Carrying lots of packages.

- Walking near parked cars, thick trees or bushes, darkened alleys or doorways.

- Taking shortcuts.

Eight Effective Actions

- Feel confident and in control.
- Walk purposefully, with body straight and head erect.
- Be alert and aware of your surroundings.
- Hold your purse close to your body and away from the street.
- Note safety landmarks.
- Have your keys ready when approaching your home or car.
- Walk against the flow of traffic.
- If you're being followed, move and attract attention.

11
PHYSICAL TECHNIQUES FOR SELF DEFENSE

In the last chapter, you learned certain basic rules of self-defense. You saw that your most powerful weapon is common sense, and you followed a two-part method of acquiring street smarts: first, learning what to avoid; then, how to act on the street.

Nowhere in this basic canon of street safety was there any mention of physical attack, or defense on your part. And for good reason. Your set of street smarts is designed to keep you from being assaulted and to enable you to escape a potential assailant. The best form of defense is always escape.

If you approach physical self-defense as a way to deal with potential aggressors, you put yourself in danger. Why? Because instead of focusing all your attention on escaping a potentially dangerous situation, you might try to win a battle with a seasoned, ruthless criminal.

Now, I am going to give you a few physical self-defense techniques to use if the unlikely happens and you are attacked. With these techniques, you can feel sure that you can defend yourself, even against a strong aggressor. But this form of defense is not easy. You have to fight not only the aggressor but also your own fear and your repulsion of violence—and that's no picnic!

Common sense (your Number-One safety tool!) states clearly that you should not go into battle with a mugger or a rapist, if at all possible. But common sense also tells you that you should be prepared to meet an attack.

How should you approach physical self-defense? In three ways:

1. Never try to fight a *potential* attacker. Try to escape from him.

2. Fight back *only* if you can't escape and your *life* (not your purse or your chastity) is in danger.

3. If you are fighting for your life, fight as hard as you can. Forget about fighting fairly.

But remember that your goal is still *escape*, not murder.

Consider the following basic self-defense techniques as you would an escape ladder. You keep it under the bed in case of fire. Since you have taken all the necessary precautions to fireproof your home, you know that it's extremely unlikely that a fire will break out, but if it should happen, you want a way of escape. That's all these techniques are— a way of escape.

Technique #1: Yell at the top of your lungs. Always do this first. If you make a wild, animal-like sound, you may actually frighten your attacker away. A wild, leonine roar ("RRAAHHH!") or a traditional karate-style yell ("AHKEYAH!") will certainly surprise him and give you time to plan your next move. Put as much force as you can into your shout—the louder it is, the more effective.

There are a few other reasons for preceding any form of self-defense with a yell. First, yelling requires taking a deep breath which, in turn, makes your abdominal muscles contract. This contraction gives your body more power to put into a physical act. Second, yelling or screaming actually prepares your body to fight. Following a hearty holler, the adrenaline flows, the blood pressure rises, the mind sharpens, and the body tenses for attack. And finally, a loud yell is a great antidote to panic. It loosens up the muscles paralyzed by fear, galvanizes you, and—at the very least—startles your assailant.

Studies of attacks on women show that more than half the women escaped unharmed just by yelling.

Technique #2: To break a wrist hold: If someone grabs your wrists from the front, snap your arms up and out against his thumbs. You should be able to free yourself quickly, as the power of your arms is likely to be greater than the power of his thumbs, no matter how strong he is. Follow with Technique 5, 6, 7, or—if necessary—8.

Technique #3: To break a strangle-hold from the front: Raise your hands to the outside of your attacker's elbows and push his elbows in. Draw back as you do this. Then move to Techniques 5 through 8, whichever are appropriate.

Technique #4: To break a strangle-hold from the back: First, turn your head in the direction of the elbow grabbing you. This will give you extra space to breathe. If you have a free arm, grab one of your assailant's fingers and try to bend it back. You'll either break the grip or his finger.

Technique #5: Kick or bite sensitive spots. Your foot is eleven times more powerful than your hand, and your jaws are very strong indeed. Aim for your attacker's most vulnerable areas. A sharp bite on the ear, nose, upper lip, or testicles can temporarily incapacitate and sometimes stun the attacker. So can a kick to those places or the kneecaps or instep.

Technique #6: The testicle squeeze. This requires a minimum of strength—but you do have to be quick or your attacker will realize what you're about to do. Grab his testicles and squeeze as hard as you can. You'll send him into shock—literally.

Technique #7: If your hands are immobilized: Stamp your heel on the top of his foot, using as much force as you can. You can do this whether the attacker is in front of or behind you. Fourteen pounds of pressure will break the bones in a foot.

Technique #8: If there's no other way. The following acts can kill, quickly. You have the right to resort to deadly force to protect your life or another's, if that life is under threat. But you don't have the right to kill a purse snatcher. The three deadly acts of self-defense are:

1. Kicking or striking the side of the assailant's neck or the front of his throat with the edge of a stiffened hand. A blow to the side of the neck can rupture a large artery. A chop on the front of the throat can make the larynx swell, causing suffocation.

2. Pushing your thumbs into his eyes. A moderate push will make him pass out, and a hard one will kill him.

3. Pressing your index fingers below the earlobes, just above the jawbone. A firm press for two seconds will send him into shock. Pressure for more than six seconds will kill him.

You can practice Techniques 3, 4, and 5 with a partner to get a feel for them. Obviously, the others can be performed only in your mind.

A knowledge of basic physical self-defense is your "disaster insurance." As in most insurance policies, the fine print is not too pleasant to read, but you need to know it.

It will improve your greatest self-defense: your self-confidence and knowlege that you can defend your own life.

Read over your checklist periodically to fix the actions in your memory for easy recall. But remember—they are your disaster insurance. Use them only as a last resort.

SAFETY CHECKS

If Your Life Is in Danger

- Yell as loudly as you can.

- To break a wrist hold from the front, snap your arms up and out against the assailant's thumbs.

- To break a stranglehold from the front, press your hands firmly on the outside of your assailant's elbows.

- To break a stranglehold from the back, turn your head in the direction of his elbow for breath, then pull back on one of his fingers.

- Kick or bite. Sensitive spots include: eyes, nose, upper lip, ears, testicles, kneecaps, instep.

- Squeeze the testicles.

- Stamp on the instep.

- Put pressure on the pressure points: side of neck, front of throat, above the jaw bones behind ears. Pressure or a hard blow on these points can stun and severe pressure can kill.

12
TRAVELING BY CAR

Many women are nervous about traveling alone by car. Why? Because they don't feel in control. They often don't know how to deal with automotive breakdowns, which can be dangerous in bad or deserted neighborhoods. And when traveling alone, they are afraid of being accosted if they're seen eating alone at a restaurant or—even worse—checking into a motel.

You don't have to be afraid—because you *can* be in control. Not only can you take the necessary precautions to make breakdowns unlikely, you can also follow up with a plan for dealing with them if they occur. And you can prepare yourself to eat and sleep along the way, in safety.

Here's how.

BASIC CAR CARE

Common sense tells us that machines break down when they are not properly maintained. You don't have to know all the workings of that maze under the hood (most men don't, either) to institute a maintenance system that will make breakdowns extremely unlikely.

To keep your car in good running order:

1. Read the operator's manual. All of it. Know what the gauges on your dashboard mean. If you don't under-stand something in the book, make a note of it and ask your dealer or mechanic to explain it to you the next time you take the car in for a checkup.

There are two reasons for reading the manual. One, you will know what to watch out for. Two, you will start to build confidence in your ability to take care of yourself in the car. In the car as on the street, bafflement makes you an easy victim. Confidence is your cloak of safety.

2. Maintain the car according to the schedule in the operator's manual. In fact, it's a good idea to take it in a little while before you've run the stated number of miles, particularly for oil changes and lubrication. Most people find that the oil gets dirty before the intervals stated in the manual.

3. Watch your gas station attendant when he checks the oil, water, and tires. Get out of the car and observe what he's doing. Note *where* to check the oil and water and remember the *level* on the stick or in the radiator that shows you need more. Look at and feel the tires when they're properly inflated. You should also buy a tire gauge and learn how to use it; then you'll be able to monitor them yourself and know when to get air.

4. Have the oil and water checked every three or four weeks—more if you drive a lot. And don't forget, you can check them yourself at home. You should do this before any long trip, but remember to test the water level before you start out. Don't try it while the engine is hot.

5. Once a week, inspect your tires for nails, glass, gouges, and tread wear. If a tire looks bad you must get it changed right away.

6. Always fill up when the tank is half full. Make this

an absolute rule. Treat the halfway mark on the gas gauge as if it were the empty mark. Running out of gas on a dark, deserted highway is practically unforgivable. You owe yourself better treatment than that.

Good maintenance means regular checks and prompt attention to your car's needs. Don't catch yourself saying day after day, "I must get that tire changed." Do it—and start enjoying the pleasure of being able to rely on yourself!

DEFENSIVE DRIVING

Defensive driving doesn't mean driving with your heart in your mouth. It means using your common sense when you drive so that you don't have to be afraid. It means taking care of yourself.

Always keep your doors locked. Police advise that you also keep your windows closed, or at least open no more than two inches. If it's a hot day and you don't have air conditioning, open your window fully and the opposite one a little, for a breeze. But always roll up the window on the driver's side at traffic lights and intersections in questionable areas of town.

Place your purse and packages under the seat, out of view, when you're driving. In that way, purse snatchers won't be tempted to reach in and grab them (if, in fact, you did leave that window down!).

If you can avoid them, do not use dark side roads at night, even in your own neighborhood. Travel on main highways and lighted streets.

Don't pick up strangers. Ever. That includes both men and women. A recent survey in Arizona showed that, out of 100 hitchhikers, there were only 4 who had no previous or current problems with the law. Incredible? But true.

If someone tries to force his way into your car, be sure the door is locked and then beep your horn intermittently to attract attention and scare him away.

Keep an eye on the cars in front of and behind you. If either one seems to be sticking too close to you, lead him to a police station, a gas station, or a well-lit restaurant. If you have no doubt that you're being followed, set up the intermittent horn blasts as you approach your destination. Get the license plate number if you can, and call the police from the place where you stop.

Always carry in your car: a flashlight that works (check periodically); flares; a white rag or hankerchief to signal for help; jumper cables for starting a dead battery (and learn how to use them—it's easy!); an inflated spare tire; a jack; and a wrench. In northern winters, be sure you're fitted with snow tires and have chains, a shovel, antifreeze, a de-icer, and a bag of sand in the trunk.

SOME EXTRA INSURANCE

You should make two valuable investments for your own safety. Join an auto club and get a citizen-band radio installed in your car.

The auto club will send you planned routes, and advise you of weather, road conditions, and sometimes recommended lodgings for any trip you wish to take. You can also call on them for emergency service, day or night, even if it's just changing a tire or helping you if you're locked out of your car. And you don't need to worry about having enough money—many services are free, or they'll bill you later.

The CB radio is your hot line to the police. Keep it set on the emergency channel. Then if you're stranded or in any kind of trouble, just sit tight in your locked car and call for help over the CB.

IF YOU HAVE A BREAKDOWN

A breakdown in a bad area or on a lonely stretch of road is

many a female driver's nightmare. It needn't be yours, because you will be in control.

If you see a gas station and your can can limp along to it, by all means do so. If you don't or can't, pull over to the side and stay in your car. Keep the windows up and the doors locked.

If you have a CB, use it to call the police for help. If not, you can open your hood and tie a white rag or handkerchief to your door handle or radio antenna. People will know you're in trouble and may stop to help. Open your window a few inches only, give the passerby money for a phone call, and ask him to call the police for you. If you don't like the look of him, thank him for stopping but tell him you've already sent for the police. He won't stick around to meet them.

If you'd rather not advertise your breakdown, stay in the car and flash the blinking lights or signal for help only when you see a police car approaching. But if the street is not well lit, it may not be easy to spot the police car.

However long it takes for help to arrive, don't get out to go looking for it. You're much safer in your car than you are walking down a dark street or deserted highway.

PARK SAFELY

Park in well-lit places. If the diner where you were intending to stop is surrounded by dark acres of parked cars or a bunch of hot rods, eat somewhere else.

Try not to park near intersections, bus stops, traffic lights, or stop signs. These are favorite stops for rapists and purse snatchers.

Always check for loiterers when you return to your car, wherever you park—even outside your friend's twenty-five-room mansion. Make sure all the doors are still locked and check out the back seat before you get in.

STAY SAFE

When you're traveling alone, it's wise to stop at well-known, standard motels and restaurants. This is not the time to experiment with the little French place someone told you about that is somewhere down a certain road.

If you're uncomfortable eating alone, bring along a good book for company. Just don't become so absorbed in it that you totally take your eyes off the people around you.

If you want a drink, you're wiser to have it at your table than alone at the bar. You're not being unliberated; you're just being smart.

When you check in at a motel, don't display a wad of cash. Whenever possible, use travelers checks or a credit card. Above all, use your common sense. Don't get into the elevator with someone who gives you "bad vibes." Don't carry so much luggage that you have to depend on strangers to help you. Do lock your door with the safety lock and chain as soon as you're in your room, and do leave a light on when you leave the room.

Reread chapter 9 to review safety tips for traveling alone. Have a safe trip! You will, now that you're in control.

SAFETY CHECKS

Car Care

- Read the operator's manual.

- Maintain the car on schedule.

- Learn how to check the oil, water, and tires.

- Have the oil and water checked every three or four weeks.

- Check your tires once a week.

- Fill up when the tank's half full.

Defensive Driving

- Keep the doors locked and the windows almost closed.

- Hide your purse and packages under the seat.

- Drive on main highways and lighted streets.

- Don't pick up strangers.

- Lead a follower to a police station, gas station, or restaurant.

- Honk horn intermittently if you're in trouble.

- Carry a flashlight, flares, white rag, jumper cables, inflated spare tire, jack, wrench, and equipment for winter driving.

Safety Insurance

- Join an auto club.

- Install a CB radio.

In Case of a Breakdown

- Stay in the car.

- Call the police over the CB.

- Signal for help with a raised hood and white rag.

Park Safely and Stay Safe

- Park in well-lit areas.

- Eat and stay in regular, crowded restaurants and motels.

- Don't flash cash; use travelers checks or credit cards.

- Double-lock your room when you're in; leave a light on when you're out.

13
TAKING PUBLIC TRANSPORTATION

So far, I've stressed the three C's of safety: using your *common sense* and feeling *confident* and in *control*. Now it's time to add another element to your safety package: *expect the unexpected.*

This should be your motto whenever you use public transportation. Most women who have had trouble on buses or trains did not expect anything to happen. They were riding a bus or train they had taken many times before on a route they knew well. The very familiarity of the vehicle and the route lulled them into heedlessness, and sometimes even into sleep. Once again, they unwittingly gave a criminal the opportunity to make them victims.

So your first rule of safety is: don't sleep in the subway—or on the bus or even on the commuter train. Expect the unexpected, from the moment you set off for the bus stop to the moment you arrive at your destination. Keep your eyes open, and you won't be caught unawares.

Here is a gathering of safety tips from experts who want you to have a safe ride:

WHEN YOU TAKE A BUS

1. Choose a bus stop that is well lit and well popu-

lated. If the stop you regularly use is dark, isolated, or used by very few people, change stops. Don't get off at a deserted stop if you can help it. Try to leave with a crowd and walk the extra distance, but only if the way is peopled and well lit.

2. Avoid waiting alone—get a bus schedule and plan to arrive at the stop only a few minutes before your bus pulls in.

3. When you're waiting for the bus, stand a few feet back from the spot where passengers get on and off. Purse snatchers sometimes hang around the bus's loading area and then reach out to grab a purse as the bus departs. If the owner holds onto her purse, she can literally be dragged along by the bus. Like so many needless crimes, this one can always be avoided by a simple precaution— stand back.

4. Have your change or token ready in your hand when you get on. You don't want to be rummaging in your purse for money when you're in a crowd.

5. Sit in the front, near the driver. Criminals favor the back of the bus, where they can threaten and rob people unseen and unheard. If you can't get a seat right by the driver, sit in an aisle seat near the exit door. Then you can leave your seat or the bus if anyone bothers you. However, take extra precautions with your purse—the seat next to the door is often the favorite of purse snatchers.

6. Hold your purse and other belongings firmly on your lap.

7. If someone tries to molest you, shout out loud "Take your hands off me!" or even, "Take your *filthy* hands off me!!" He'll stop. If you're too embarrassed to make a scene like this, he may decide to follow you home.

8. Get off at different stops and if possible vary your route home. Robbers and rapists look for regular patterns to follow. Don't give them one.

9. Check to see who's getting off the bus with you. If you spot an unsavory-looking character, you may prefer to stay on until the next stop.

WHEN YOU RIDE THE SUBWAY AND TRAIN

Follow the guidelines for bus travel, and add the following:

1. Always wait in a lighted area. At the subway station, stand near the token booth. If someone is bothering you, tell the person in the booth and ask him or her to call the police.

2. Never stand at the edge of the platform or approach it until the train has come to a complete stop in the station.

3. If you're not sure which train you need, ask a policeman or transit employee—not another passenger.

4. If you can, sit in the front car near the driver. If not, choose a car with several people in it. Always avoid the last car—it's the preferred site of subway crime.

5. If you're not sitting near the driver, choose a seat near the door. (Remember to hold on to your purse!) Then you can easily slip out if a group of undesirable-looking people enters your car. Glance at the station first; if it's empty, plan to get off at the next stop. When you do leave, do so quickly and unobtrusively, just as the door shuts.

6. Always move forward if your car empties.

7. If anyone in the train disturbs you, go up to a transit officer and tell him. If there's no public official around, scream and pull the emergency cord. Don't imagine that screaming should be saved for life-threatening emergencies. Loud noise is anathema to criminals, who like to do their work in quiet; screaming can often prevent a life-threatening emergency.

8. Try not to take public transportation—especially subways—late at night. See if a friend will give you a ride home, or take a taxi.

If you follow these few safety precautions, you will outwit the "land sharks" lurking on public transportation—and reach your destination safely.

SAFETY CHECKS

- Stay alert and always expect the unexpected.

- Get a schedule and plan to arrive just a minute or two before the bus or train pulls in.

- Wait for your bus or train in a lighted, crowded area, near a public transport official if possible.

- Don't stand right near the entrance to the bus or train.

- Have your money or token ready in your hand.

- Sit near the driver or near a door.

- Stand away from the edge of the subway platform.

- On the subway, avoid the back car and any car with only one or two people in it.

- Hold your purse and packages firmly on your lap.

- If someone bothers you, move; get off the bus or train; tell an official; or scream and pull the cord.

- Vary your route to and from work.

- Try not to use public transportation late at night.

14
MOB SCENES

They're not recommended. Any safety expert will tell you that a mob scene is a pickpocket's paradise. Some add darkly that you're lucky if that's the worst that happens to you in such a situation.

But—there's Rio and the Carnival...and Times Square on New Year's Eve...and the Rose Bowl Parade...and so many other exciting, memorable events that are, by nature, mob scenes. In fact, the crowd is part of the fun! And probably, at least once in your life, you're going to want to be there.

There are other times when you may find yourself unexpectedly caught up in a mob scene—during a breakdown on a train, or at the scene of an accident, or in a crush at a football game. You might even end up right in the middle of a street riot.

What can you do to keep safe?

IF YOU KNOW YOU'RE GOING TO BE IN A CROWD

First—get yourself a money belt and leave your purse at home. You don't have to carry around a comb or makeup.

Opening a bag to fix your hair or lipstick is definitely not a good idea in a crowd scene. All you really need with you is a little money and some identification tucked into the money belt with the purse inside, against your body.

The key as far as clothing is concerned is simplicity and function. Wear something that doesn't impede your movements and that doesn't make you stand out as particularly robbable or rapable. In other words, leave both your sable coat and your skin-tight jeans at home.

Comfortable, low-heeled shoes let you move freely. If you want to get away from the people around you, backless, spike-heeled sandals are about as much help as a rope around your ankles. And, don't wear expensive jewelry or heavy chain-type necklaces or bracelets.

If someone nearby tries anything, say loudly, "Get your hands off me!" He may look around innocently, and you may look like a fool—but whom are you trying to impress? You can always move away to another area afterward. If you just move quietly away, it's likely that the cause of your discomfort may follow you.

If you can't get up the courage to confront your molester so openly, simply say loudly, "Someone's pushing me." The crowd will naturally move back—and your troublemaker probably won't want to show up as the limpet that sticks.

If you didn't wear a money belt and you feel someone's hand in your pocket or grabbing your purse, point to the escaping thief and yell, "He's got my wallet!" If the crowd is thick, he won't be able to get far, and the people around you will tend to close in and help you recover your property.

As a final precaution for guarding against close-up offenders, you might decide to pin a hat pin to your sleeve. It can put a very effective stop to greedy hands or unwelcome advances.

IF YOU FIND YOURSELF CAUGHT IN A MOB SCENE

It is very important not to panic. If you are in the middle of a congested area—especially indoors—one of your serious problems may be not getting enough air. If you start gasping and gulping in terror, you'll increase your need for air. Stay calm, try to breathe normally, and plan your best escape route.

First, you should try to get as far away as possible from the source of the trouble. Concentrate on edging carefully to the outside of the crowd. The farther you are from the boiling center, the lower will be the level of heat, activity, and possible danger.

If you're caught in a street riot, make for a place where you can get off the street. As soon as you can, go into the nearest public building. Once you're inside, continue to move inward and upward. Your goal is to get away from all low-level windows and doors, through which rocks, bullets, and explosives can easily fly.

When you reach a safe room, barricade the door and, if possible, push a large, heavy object against the window. Resist the temptation to watch the mayhem from a window, even an upper-story one. By silhouetting yourself against the window, you become a target for a crazed fanatic's rifle or hand grenade. If you must look out of the window, stand to one side and glance quickly. Then stay out of the line of fire. The police will let you know when all's clear.

SAFETY CHECKS

When You Know There's Going to Be a Crowd

- Put your money and ID in a money belt.

- Wear easy-fitting, unobtrusive clothes.

- Don't wear expensive jewelry or heavy chains around your neck or wrists.

- If someone bothers you, announce loudly what he or she is doing—then move.

- Pin a precautionary hat pin to your sleeve.

In a Riot or Other Dangerous Mob Scene

- Keep calm.

- Edge away from the eye of the storm.

- Get into the nearest public building.

- Move upward and inward, staying away from windows and doors.

- Barricade yourself inside a room.

- Stay there.

15

ATTACK BY ANIMALS

Probably the only "wild animal" you're concerned about avoiding is the lone wolf of the human species. But it's wise to protect yourself against four-legged animals, too.

For one thing, you want to be free to live as you want to live and go where you want to go. By knowing how to treat different types of animals, you may feel easier about taking a more adventurous vacation or even walking down the street past that frightening Doberman.

WOMAN'S BEST FRIEND—SOMETIMES

First, let's look at the most familiar friend or foe: the neighborhood dog. If you've ever lived near a vicious dog, you know how tyrannizing it can be. For years, I didn't dare walk around my own house for fear of encountering "Janus," a local Siberian husky who bared his teeth, growled, rushed up to me, and snapped at my heels and legs as soon as he saw me. His eighty-five-year-old owner should have kept him off the streets—but she didn't. And we all knew that removal of Janus by the police could have serious effects on his owner, for which none of us wanted to be responsible. So, Janus made us prisoners in our own homes.

Then there was the time I was chased into the sea by a dog whose owner wanted to keep "her beach" free of intruders. The beach was public property but who was going to argue with a snarling German shepherd?

You may encounter an unfriendly dog in any number of situations, and you don't have to be cowed.

First of all, be sure to avoid provoking the dog. Don't run away the minute you see him; you'll induce him to follow. Walk briskly and look self-assured. Like a criminal, a dog can read your signals of confidence, and they may actually inspire a little fear in him.

It goes without saying that you should never taunt, tease, or willfully upset any animal. Anyone who does will ultimately provoke the animal to attack—and will probably receive little help from bystanders, whose sympathies may rightly be with the dog.

But let's assume that you did nothing to incite the dog and he turns on you anyway. Your first response should be the same one you bring to any aggressor: *don't panic*. But, in this situation that means: *don't scream*. Dogs, even nasty ones, are not criminals! Screaming won't frighten them away. On the contrary, they'll know that you are afraid of them and that, therefore, they are the ones in control.

Tell yourself firmly that you are in charge. The dog will pick up your feeling of self-assurance, just as he picks up feelings of fear.

Now, even when they're on the attack, dogs frequently respond quickly to commands. "Down," "Stay," or "Sit" are familiar commands to most dogs. Once you've quelled your own panic, look the dog straight in the eyes and give him one of those well-known commands in a loud, decisive, and imperative tone of voice.

Don't yell, "Go away!" or "Leave me alone!" These are not familiar commands to most dogs. You are trying to use a word that will set off a reflex action—namely, obedience. Unfamiliar commands simply won't do the trick.

If the dog does not respond to your command and continues to rush at you, don't run unless you can quickly escape behind a door (which you would immediatley lock) or up a tree. An angry dog can run very fast, and your flight will spur him on to the hunt.

Instead, try to fend him off by wrapping your coat or sweater over your arm and holding that arm in front of you. Keep using commands. Or, if you have a canister of tear gas with you (see Weapons in the Appendix), spray it into his face. You can then run away fast while he's crippled by temporary blindness. If he still attacks, try to knock his head aside and kick his throat until he runs away.

If he fastens his mouth onto any part of your body or your clothing, don't pull back. He'll only sink his teeth in deeper. Do the opposite: Lean in the same direction he's pulling in and kick his throat until he lets go. Continue to kick until he runs away.

When a dog absolutely cannot be subdued (it's rare, but it happens—particularly if he's been "set upon you" by someone like my crazy beach-lady), you can protect yourself from serious injury by falling to the ground face down, with your hands clasped behind your neck. Keep your legs tight together and press your elbows and stomach hard against the ground. In this position, you make it impossible for the dog to reach your throat or any vital organ.

Practice that fall a few times at home to make it part of your safety reflexes. And remember, the teeth of most dogs are too short to cause really dangerous wounds, and their claws are too blunt to scratch deeply.

Should you be bitten by a dog, the animal must be checked for rabies as soon as possible. If this is not done, you must assume that it is rabid and go for a series of treatments. If you know who owns the dog, tell them immediately and see that they get it checked. Call the police if they don't, or if you don't recognize the dog; report its appearance and the location of the attack.

CREATURES OF THE WILD

Most wild animals do not attack unless they are provoked. They don't want human contact. What they do want is to be left alone and unharmed. If neither you nor your pet nor your child bothers them—you can be pretty sure they won't bother you.

Your best protection from wild animals is to enjoy them from a distance. Specifically:

1. Don't approach a baby animal until you have watched for a long time to see that it is, in fact, abandoned. Your cooings to the baby won't be appreciated by a large mother lurking in the background. Of course, if you see a young animal in trouble, with no parent coming to its aid, you have to help. Don some heavy overclothes and gloves if you can. And call a vet for advice.

2. Keep your dog on a leash if you go into wild country. In that way you won't have to extricate it from unpleasant encounters with wild animals.

3. On an evening walk in autumn, don't shuffle through piles of leaves. They are favorite resting places for spiders, rodents, scorpions, and snakes.

4. Don't sneak up on a large wild animal to get a close-up photograph. Not a few amateur shutterbugs have been killed by their subjects.

5. Avoid any mammal that is acting peculiarly. Don't just walk away; run. Rabies is still rampant in the United States, with skunks being the principal carriers.

6. Keep food, drink, and perfumed substances locked up in the trunk of the car if you're out camping or hiking. Don't invite unwelcome guests to dinner!

If, despite these precautions, you are ever attacked by a wild animal, handle the situation as you would a dog attack. A canister of tear gas can be good protection if you're really venturing into the wilds.

SAFETY CHECKS

To Avoid Attack

- Enjoy all strange animals from a distance.

- Don't go near a baby animal until you've checked whether the mother is near.

- Keep your dog on a leash.

- Stay away from piles of leaves.

- Move quickly away from any animal that acts in a bizarre manner.

- When hiking or camping, lock food, drink, and perfumed substances in trunk.

In Case of Attack

- Keep calm and tell yourself you're in control.

- Command an aggressive dog: *Sit, Stay,* or *Down.*

- Fend off an attack with your covered arm or tear gas.

- Lean into a bite; don't pull away. Have dog tested for rabies if possible; if you can't get the animal, go for rabies treatments yourself.

- Kick the animal's throat to loosen hold.

- If you can't subdue the attacker, lie face down, with your hands over your neck and your body pressed against the ground.

VIOLENT CRIME
PART 4

16
SURVIVING RAPE

Rape. It's the crime you don't want to think about—and the one that springs to your mind the moment you find yourself alone on a dark street. It's the horror you read about and tell yourself you'd never survive—and then put out of your mind because it's hard even to survive thinking about it.

And it's a few other things as well: It's a crime that is more likely to happen in your own home than any other place; it's a crime committed by "friends," relatives, and acquaintances as well as by strangers; and it's a crime that isn't reported over 90 percent of the time.

Most important of all—it's a crime that you can control. Not always perfectly. You may take all the safety precautions and still find yourself in the clutches of a rapist, but you will still have some control. There are techniques for escaping that you can use—but only if your life is not threatened. Even if you can't escape, you can control rape's effect on you. You can survive. You can go on leading a good life.

This last point is the most important. Rape *is* horrible, it *is* the ultimate violation, it *can* and probably will lead to nightmares. But if you're emotionally and psychologically prepared, you can live through it because you can stay in control of your own reactions and refuse to be destroyed.

There are many books about rape. Some stress the victim's legal rights, others possible techniques of self-defense, others the implications of rape in our society today. But, what we're concerned with here is your safety, and all the experts and the studies are in agreement on certain crucial areas:

- What to do to avoid rape
- What to do to escape rape
- What to do if you can't escape
- What to do to survive with pride

These are the techniques we will look at in this chapter.

WAYS TO AVOID RAPE

1. Be Aware. Wherever you are, remember that you are literally your own bodyguard. Don't sleep, dream, or read to the point of becoming oblivious to your surroundings in public places. Always notice who's near you and whether there's anyone else around. For instance, passengers on a bus or train tend to choose seats surrounded by empty ones. If a man ignores the empty seats and comes to sit right next to you, be on your guard. Plan to get off fast at the next stop, before he realizes what you're doing. If ever your intuition says beware, listen to it and *move*.

2. Dress to prevent rape. Studies show that rapists don't discriminate; any woman is a possible target. Anyone who tells a rape victim that she was "asking for it" by the way she dressed is not only ignorant but insensitive. Yet common sense has something to say, too. Short skirts, see-through blouses, and tight jeans simply are not good protection against sexual assault. So go ahead and wear whatever you like around people you know and trust—but when you're alone or with someone you're not sure of—use your common sense. Be liberated enough not to have to prove it!

3. Don't reveal your name, telephone number, or any personal habits to a stranger who calls. A rapist's favorite ploy is to randomly dial a number and then, if a woman answers, ask for someone else. When told he has the wrong number, he then says, "Who's this?" The woman tells him. He then says, "I was trying to reach 234-5678 (or whatever). What number is this, please?" And the woman gives him her number. He now has her name and number and can look up her address in the phone book. (A good reason not to list your address in the phone book!)

Another trick rapists use is a "telephone survey." Pretending to be doing research, they try to get you to tell them about your habits: how you go to work, when you get home, and so on. Refuse to be a part of any such "survey." Just say you won't answer and hang up. If the calls persist, call the police.

4. Don't go to the laundry room of your apartment building or any other lonely place alone at night. I have mentioned this before, but it's worth repeating here in case you turned to this chapter first! Rapists and robbers don't like crowds. They like deserted spots, such as laundry rooms at night, where no one is likely to get between them and their prey.

5. Don't wait at isolated bus stops or train stations. You have read this before, too, but it has special importance here. Remember, a rapist's haunts are dark, lonely places. Stay out of them.

6. If a car behind you starts flashing its headlights,

keep on moving. Don't, please, get taken in by this old trick of a criminal pretending to be a police officer. If a police car is signaling you to pull over, you will see a flashing blue-and-red light on its roof, and you may hear its siren. You can be sure that a car flashing its regular lights at you is not a police car. Do not stop for it. If the driver keeps bothering you by driving beside you or continuously flashing his lights, try to get his license plate number and then drive to the nearest gas station and call the police.

7. If someone tries to get in your car at a traffic light or stop sign, sound horn intermittently. You'll get the attention of onlookers, if there are any. (Remember —if people hear a steady, unending horn they will probably think it's stuck and not pay attention.) If the intruder doesn't go away, drive ahead, even on a red light, as long as you're not endangering anyone. Don't worry about breaking the law; this is one time you want to attract the police's attention. If the person gets in before you can drive away, scream, turn on the car's inside light, sound the horn, and open or break a window.

8. Read Chapters 1, 5, 8–13. The safety tips given there will further help you protect yourself against rape.

COLLEGE CAMPUSES

It's a sad fact that college campuses attract rapists. The isolation, deserted pathways, late-night hours, empty buildings, and young women walking alone—back from the library, to an evening class, home from a party—all add up to an abundance of opportunities for a rapist to find a victim. Your common sense is never more important than when you're living at college.

The first rule of safety is: *Never* walk alone at night. Most colleges have escort services; if yours doesn't, contact the campus security office or dean and organize such a service. Then, of course, you must use it, *always*. In addition to escort services, many colleges have instituted a whistle system under which every woman carries a "rape whistle" on her key chain—if any strange man should approach you, blow the whistle and people will come to your rescue.

You also must be particularly aware of avoiding deserted places. These include poorly-lit shortcuts—stick to populated thoroughfares—and college libraries, which often contain many rooms that are empty—don't study there! Always stay in a room with at least five or six people; in that way you won't have to switch rooms in the middle of your studies if a few people leave. And, never venture into the laundry room late at night. If your dorm has community bathrooms down the hall there should be an inside lock to use at night. Ask for one if there isn't.

Treat your dorm room as you would an apartment. Always lock the door when you leave, even if it's only to run down the hall to make a phone call or borrow something from a friend. Make sure all the windows are securely closed and the blinds or drapes are drawn at night. There may be safety in numbers, but dormitories also offer a variety of means for an assailant to get in and hide. Your dormitory should have a meeting at least once every few months to review dorm security.

And most importantly, go to the meetings your college holds about rape. You'll learn about the safety problems of your particular environment as well as the safety measures — such as outside alarms, the whistle system, and so forth —that your college has instituted to protect you.

WHAT TO DO TO ESCAPE RAPE

Experts advise two initial strategies. The first is to stay alert and competent and the second, talk to your assailant. Let's look at these two in some detail.

1. Show competence. The rapist expects you to be a passive victim, overwhelmed by his terrifying presence to the point of being paralyzed by fear. If you are not, you may very well throw him into confusion. Women who have met rapists with an alert, competent air have reported that this response has actually sent the assailant away.

2. Talk to your assailant. This may seem extraordinarily difficult—but it works. Without getting into a long discussion of the psychology of the rapist, I'll tell you why.

Rapists are, by definition, sick. Most of them approach rape not as an outlet for an overactive sex drive but as a violent means of achieving supremacy by subduing another person. In an article in *The American Journal of Psychiatry* ("Rape: Power, Anger and Sexuality," November 1977) rape is defined as "a pseudosexual act in which the rapist is much more concerned with status, aggression, control and dominance over the victim than with receiving sexual gratification."

To commit rape, the rapist needs to perceive himself as a vicious, powerful being who may be hated but cannot be overcome. And he needs to see his victim as different from himself. She is weak—while he is strong. She is a helpless female—he is a powerful male. She is the passive "accepter" he the active assailant; she is the prey, he the predator. In other words, the rapist needs to see his victim as someone who is not connected to him in any way except one: She plays the victim to his victor. In that way alone, they complement each other.

Now, when you talk to him as one human being to another, you change the script completely. If you can make the rapist feel different about himself and his relation to you, you may be able to avoid rape. There have been many reports of women who literally talked themselves out of a potential rape. By treating the rapist as a human being similar to themselves whom they could actually like and respect, they somehow made him switch gears, calm down, and, eventually, leave them alone.

One grandmother confronted by a young rapist in her kitchen told him he reminded her of her grandson. He turned around and fled.

Other women have been successful with a very different approach. They talked seductively and invitingly and pretended to go along with the rapist's sexual demands. Once the assailant's guard was down, they escaped.

One young woman cornered in a dark alley told her assailant how attractive he was. She went on to say that she'd very much like him to make love to her, "but—not here!" This self-possessed woman was able to persuade her would-be attacker to come back to her apartment with her. Once they reached the crowded foyer, she screamed for help and got him arrested!

In his far-ranging study of rape, *How to Say No to a Rapist*, Frederic Storaska says communication is the primary component in successfully foiling a rape attempt.

But what if talking doesn't work—or you're just too scared to do it?

3. Try to escape if the assailant is not threatening your life. Repeat, *not* threatening your life. If the rapist is threatening you, attempting to escape can be extremely dangerous. Your life is more important than your chastity. Some ways of escape are:

- Try to repel him by saying you have a venereal disease, cancer, or menstrual cramps. Or act crazy: Start babbling or drooling. Stick your finger down your throat to induce vomiting, or fake an epileptic fit.

- If you're not in a deserted place, yell, "FIRE!!" That brings people; "HELP!" doesn't.

- Make him, not you, remove your clothing. While his hands are occupied, run.

- Break his hold, using one of the techniques discussed in chapter 11.

WHAT TO DO
IF YOU CAN'T ESCAPE

1. If your life is being threatened, submit to the rape. Why? Because most rapists intend to rape, not kill. After committing the rape, they disappear. According to the National Commission on the Causes and Prevention of Violence, 75 percent of the victims of reported rapes are *not* physically hurt.

However, rapists are often crazed people who will kill a woman whom they have threatened, if she continues to resist or tries to escape. Don't take chances with your life —in this case, fighting back could kill you.

2. If your life is threatened after the rape, fight back as hard and as viciously as you can. The key word here is *after* the rape, and only as a last resort. You are little match for a strong, armed, crazy criminal who has much practice in violence and no respect for human life. That's why you should submit to the rapist, because there's a good chance that it will stop him from threatening your life. But—people who know they're fighting for their lives can draw on extra reserves of strength. Tell yourself that you're going to *win* this battle, even if you have to kill or maim your antagonist to do so. If that's difficult, ask yourself what you'd do if he were threatening your child or someone you love. Well, that's just what he's doing by threatening you.

Then scream at the top of your lungs and do any of the following—whichever you can:

- Push your thumbs sharply into his eyes.

- Press the point behind the ears where the jaw meets the skull.

- Ram your thumbs into his neck and press as hard as you can.

- Squeeze his testicles as hard as you can (you don't need a lot of strength to make an assailant pass out with this technique).

- Bash his temple, nose, throat, or Adam's apple with a sharp or heavy object or, failing that, the side of your hand.

- Bite anything you can. (Yes, anything. One woman foiled an attempt at forced oral sex this way, and she sent the rapist howling into the night.) You can disable an attacker by fierce, hard bites on the fingers, nose, toes, ears, cheeks, and throat.

- Finally, kick, stomp with your heel, pinch, elbow, rake your fingernails across his face, twist his ears, squeeze, scratch, ram an object down his throat—have no mercy and put your compunctions on hold. Don't stop at anything to save your life.

The rule is simple. Don't use physical force unless you have no alternative. If you have to use it, don't stop at anything.

WHAT TO DO
TO SURVIVE WITH PRIDE

There is a certain procedure to follow after a rape. It consists of basic steps you can take to safeguard your own health as well as apprehend the criminal.

Before you do anything else, however, your first

responsibility is to yourself. You do not have to become one of rape's marred-for-life victims. Instead of quaking in horror at what happened, congratulate yourself that you are still alive. Tell yourself that no one has the power to destroy you, especially not a deluded criminal, and keep your chin up high. Don't be afraid to tell people what happened—and don't let any stupid, misguided remarks make you feel "guilty" or "wrong." Although the law and the social climate are changing in favor of female victims, however, you still can't always count on encountering a reasonable judge or police officer. Just keep giving yourself the tremendous credit you deserve—and others soon will, too.

1. Remember that no criminal can destroy you. You are much more than your physical body because your human spirit is invulnerable to physical assault. Rape is no different from any other violent crime. It's horrible, frightening, disgusting, painful—but not demeaning. You are the same whole, worthwhile, lovable person you always were. Rape cannot destroy you unless you let it, because you can choose your own response to rape.

2. Decide whether you want to prosecute. Most books on rape advise going straight to the police. But you should know that the decision is up to you. You do not have to prosecute. But, just reporting the crime does not mean you also have to prosecute immediately; and later, when you are calmer, is probably a better time to make this decision. If you don't report the crime right away, however, you'll severely limit your chances of a successful prosecution.

Why would you want to report the rape? Probably, in the hope that justice will be done. You must report the assault if you want the criminal who hurt you to be caught and punished. And, of equal importance, you may prevent him from attacking someone else. Also, if you report the rape, you may be eligible to receive victim's financial compensation from your state.

But there may be reasons not to prosecute, usually because you don't want to go over the whole dreadful experience with law enforcement officers and then again in court—although, discussing it openly can actually act as a catharsis, particularly if you have a member of a rape crisis center with you all the time (more on that in a minute). You also may shy away because of the necessity of physical evidence. When you report, you must alert the police and then go straight to a hospital emergency room to be examined. You may not douche or clean up in any way, since then you would destroy evidence of the man's sperm or blood. And you may feel this is asking just too much of you after all you've been through. But taking along a friend or a member of a rape crisis center can make this process a lot easier for you.

Remember, your first responsibility in this case is to yourself. The rape is finished. What is the best thing you can do for yourself, now? Many women find that exercising their legal rights in order to see that justice is done provides a sense of power as well as protection in the face of a crime that usually leaves you feeling alone and vulnerable. But if it's more important for your peace of mind to get the whole thing over with as soon as possible, don't. Whatever you decide, don't feel guilty about your decision. It's your well-being that counts.

3. If you want to prosecute, call the police. They will take an initial report and then arrange for you to meet with special officers in a few days. Ask a friend or relative to stay with you at all times—you needn't feel alone. Be sure to get the names and serial numbers of all the officers who question you. If it will be easier for you (and it usually is), request a female police officer. Try to answer the questions factually and unemotionally. If you object to a question, demand to know why it is being asked. Maintain your dignity and composure and in return you will get respect.

For more on the nature of your legal rights and possible legal proceedings, turn to chapter 19.

4. Go to the hospital emergency room. This is absolutely essential, whether or not you decide to report it. You will need a complete physical examination to see if you require medical care. Describe to the doctors exactly what occurred, in detail. You may want your family doctor to be present. If you are not going to report the rape, you should go straight to your own doctor instead of to the hospital.

Be sure to have tests made for venereal disease, and check with the doctor for results in three to four days. You can also ask for preventive medicine to ward off VD. You must have the tests repeated in a couple of weeks, as some types of VD don't show up right away.

Also be sure to have a pregnancy test. Most rape victims do not become pregnant, so you should use caution and common sense in deciding what to do. You can get medication to avoid becoming pregnant, but such medication brings with it some serious health risks. Your other option is to wait to see if you are pregnant and consider a D&C or a menstrual extraction then. Ask your doctor for advice.

You also need a follow-up appointment about two weeks later for a second gonorrhea and pregnancy test, and a second follow-up four weeks after that to test for syphillis. These examinations are critical to your health.

5. Contact your local rape crisis center. It's a good idea to do this even before you go to the emergency room. The people at these centers understand what you are going through and are there to help. Most importantly, they will almost always send someone to be with you—at home, during the medical exam, during the police interview, or whenever you want.

To find your local rape crisis center, look under Rape in the white pages. You can get a free list of rape crisis centers across the country from:

The Center for Women Policy Studies
2000 P Street N.W.
Suite 508
Washington, DC 20036

If there is no rape crisis center near you, call the nearest hot line for victims of rape. These hot lines operate twenty-four hours a day, and some will accept a collect call.

You will find a list of rape hot lines across the nation in the Appendix to this book.

To get a quick referral to an appropriate psychological counselor, doctor, or lawyer, you can also call:

The National Organization for the
Prevention of Rape and Assault (NOPRA)
777 U.N. Plaza
New York, NY 10017
(212) 371-3664

SAFETY CHECKS

To Avoid Rape

- Always be aware.

- Dress wisely.

- Don't tell a stranger on the phone your name, number, or personal habits.

- Don't go to any deserted place at night.

- Don't wait at an isolated bus stop or train station.

- Don't stop for a car flashing its headlights.

- If someone tries to get in your car, honk the horn intermittently.

- Follow the safety tips in chapters 1, 5, 8–13.

To Escape Rape

- Look competent and alert.

- Talk to the rapist.

- If your life is not being threatened:

  —Say or do something repellent.
  —If people are near, yell, "FIRE!"
  —While the man is removing your clothing, run.
  —Break his hold (check chapter 11).

If You Can't Escape

- Sacrifice your chastity to save your life.

- If your life is still threatened, fight to kill.

To Survive with Pride

- Remind yourself: no criminal can destroy me.

- Decide whether you want to prosecute.

- If so, call the police.

- Go to the hospital emergency room or a doctor

- Contact your local rape crisis center for support.

17
ROBBERY

If you have followed the safety precautions suggested for protection at home, on the street, and while traveling, the chances of your being robbed are small. That's a statistical fact. Nevertheless, you still should know what to do in the face of one of those small chances!

You should have a method for dealing with every type of crime. Then, in the unlikely event that you are assaulted in any way, your method will automatically flash into your mind. If you haven't thought about and planned for a crime, you'll have no plan to draw on when you need it most.

A plan is simply a method to reach a goal; so, before you form a plan, you need to know your goal. This may sound elementary, but the wrong goal is probably the greatest reason for serious injury or even death as a result of robbery.

Anyone who comes face to face with a mugger, robber, or burglar and believes that her goal is to save her belongings is courting disaster. The man who held up a woman behind a hospital demanded her wallet. She replied, "Over my dead body!" She described the scene weakly from her bed in the emergency room, and some time later, she died of internal injuries. The wallet she had fought to keep contained $5.

$5,000 wouldn't have been worth dying for.

IN A MUGGING OR ROBBERY

1. Think: I must protect myself. That is your goal. *You* are your most valuable possession. Don't ever forget that.

2. Keep calm and look competent. That appearance may even flummox the criminal enough to send him elsewhere. He expects you to be in a panic. But the main point is: Don't make any hasty or frightened movements. If a robber thinks you are trying to reach for a weapon, he may attack you instantly. If you are held up, leave your hands exactly where they are unless you are told to hand over your wallet.

3. Don't resist. I know it sounds outrageous—telling you to turn over your own belongings meekly to some lout just because he threatens you. But look at it this way—if you dropped that same wallet out of the window of a small plane, 200 feet up, would you jump out to get it? Your chances of saving your property and yourself are about the same in a criminal holdup.

Why not scream, yell, try to escape? Because he can catch you and silence you very quickly. The time for screaming and running is *before* the confrontation, if you sense danger nearby and know that there are people close enough to hear you or there is a place to which you can escape. When you're actually accosted, it's time to change plans—do not resist!

The Denver Anti-Crime Council made an extensive study of street crime and found that running or attempting to run away during a robbery makes your chances of injury

5 times greater. Physical resistance on your part increases your chances of injury 3.7 times.

If the criminal asks for your wallet, produce it quickly. It is probably all he wants. Let it be all you lose.

4. Communicate. Many experts advise victims of holdups to treat the mugger like a rational human being and discuss the "transaction" reasonably with him. They suggest that you hand over your wallet, but then say, "Take my money, but may I keep my identification?" In this way, you show him you know the rules of the game and intend to follow them; the robber has nothing to fear. You also hold on to the documents that would give him your address.

Of course, you have to do what you feel most comfortable doing. If you know you're going to sound terrified, keep quiet. Just determine to look competent and in control and hand over your wallet or watch quietly.

5. If he threatens you, feign frailty. If people are approaching, you can fall down, pretending to faint. If you're alone, try one of these ploys: Say you have a bad heart; announce that you're pregnant; throw yourself to the floor in a hysterical fit or act absolutely insane. You may amaze him enough to send him away.

6. If he still threatens you, fight back. Again, it's always your last resort. Fighting with a violent criminal is *dangerous*. But if you're fighting for your life—scream, bite, scratch, kick, and tell yourself you're going to win. For specific defense moves, look at chapters 11 and 16.

IN A BURGLARY

If you come face-to-face with the burglar, follow the advice given above. Here are some additional tips that may help you.

1. If you suspect a break-in, get out. The moment your eye falls on something suspicious, get out of the house as quickly as possible. Call the police from a neighbor's house. Again, your goal is to protect yourself, and the best way to do this is by avoiding confrontation with the burglar.

2. If you hear someone in the house at night, yell. Call out as loudly as you can, "Bob, there's someone in the house! I'll call the police!" As you shout this, lock your bedroom door. If you've got a burglar alarm that he's somehow eluded, push the panic button in your room and *do* call the police.

3. If you walk in on a burglar in your house, pretend you think he's a repairman. This calls for composure. Say something like, "Oh, you're here already. I'm sorry, I didn't expect you this morning. Did you find the leak?" If he's got all your things strewn around—some packed into pillowcases (their favorite style of luggage)— apologize for the state of the house and ask him if he's checked the ceiling in the kitchen. Try to look completely unconcerned.

This technique gives the burglar the opportunity to escape undetected—he thinks. If you can do it casually, note his appearance (distinguishing marks, type of build, how much taller he is than you, clothes).

When he leaves, lock all doors and windows, but don't touch anything else. Go to the window to see how he leaves. If he's running, note the direction. If he goes to a car, get its license plate number. Then call the police. Give them your address, a description of the burglar, and his mode and route of escape.

4. If the burglar tries to tie you up and make off with your belongings, don't resist. Remember your goal: to save yourself. Your life is worth more than all the family heirlooms in the world. And if he does tie you up, you can take comfort in the fact that tying you up is most likely all he is going to do.

SAFETY CHECKS

To Keep Safe in a Mugging or Holdup

- Think: I must protect myself.

- Keep calm and look competent.

- Don't resist.

- Communicate.

- If he threatens you, feign frailty.

- If he still threatens you, fight back.

To Keep Safe in a Break-in

- Follow the above plan.

- If you suspect a break-in, get out.

- If you hear someone in the house at night, yell.

- If you walk in on a burglar, pretend you think he's a repairman.

- If he tries to tie you up, don't resist.

18
RANDOM VIOLENCE

Measured by the standards of a whole person—a rational human being with mental and spiritual dimensions intact—no criminal is really sane. And any act of violence against another person is an act of insanity.

But there are cases where the senselessness of the crime seems more obvious: in particular, crimes committed by the mentally disturbed or substance-addicted people who appear to attack for no reason.

Paradoxically, these people are not always the most dangerous of criminals. The cool, rational, level-headed gangster who calmly murders and maims for money or power is often much less open to negotiation than a crazed drug addict or a man mad for revenge.

The important thing to remember, no matter who is endangering you, is that you are never completely powerless. There are three valuable techniques that you can employ to minimize your danger in the face of seemingly random violence.

1. Be very calm and speak softly. Wild panic on your part will only enflame your assailant even more. A calm, steady gaze and a soft voice are like water poured over flames.

2. Look straight into your assailant's eyes and think of him as a good person. Impossible, you're screaming inside? No. All attackers are sick, but this one is obviously so. You wouldn't consider a person evil because he had cancer. The mentally disturbed or substance-addicted person is a victim of a different type of disease.

Now, you can sometimes alleviate the symptoms of that disease by giving the deranged person a sense of his own inner goodness, nobility, and self-worth. If you remember that he is sick, not evil, and determine to look at him as a fellow human being, worthy of your respect, you may defuse his rage. The efficacy of this technique has been reported time and time again.

3. Use shock tactics. A deranged person is usually clouded or confused. If techniques 1 and 2 have not calmed your assailant, do something unexpected. A quick, sudden movement, a piercing scream, a tremendous noise, a blow to the eyes, or a stamp on the foot may throw him completely off course and give you the time to escape.

Your best protection against any such confrontation is to be aware—always. Don't remain alone with someone you have funny feelings about, man or woman. And follow the advice in the chapters on safety in and outside your home.

SAFETY CHECKS

- Be very calm and speak softly.

- Look at the "good person" inside the assailant.

- If all else fails, use shock tactics.

19

GETTING HELP

No matter what happens to threaten your safety or harm you, there's always valuable help around. If you've been victimized, all you need to do is reach out. This chapter covers the services that can help you and explains your legal rights as the victim of a crime or mishap.

CALLING THE POLICE OR THE FIRE DEPARTMENT

A little forethought can halt vast amounts of crime and destruction. Read the following suggestions carefully and, if there's any preparation you haven't made, do it now. That simple act may save your life or your home.

1. Write the number of your local police and fire departments on every phone in your house. Use a label and stick it on a part of the phone where it's least likely to come off. Do the same for every phone in the house; you don't know where you'll be if you need help.

2. Memorize the numbers, especially the one for the police. You won't have your glasses on in the middle of the night! Your nervousness in a crisis may make you misread a number and waste vital time. Starting tonight, glance at the numbers and repeat them to yourself ten times. By the end of the month, you'll have them well memorized.

3. Find out where your neighbor's phone is. In an emergency, you may not have time for civilities. You may have to rush into that house and use the phone. You don't want to waste precious minutes looking for it.

4. Find out where your nearest public phone is. Your neighbor may be out. Both your neighbors may be out. And since you probably cannot afford the time it takes to race around town looking for a phone, find your nearest public phone now.

5. Remember that you can call the operator and get help. If you are in a strange place and don't know the numbers of the police or fire departments, dial "0" and say, "Police, emergency" or "Fire, emergency." The operator will put you through.

6. Before anything else, tell the police or fire department where you are and what is happening. All other information can follow. You want them to dispatch someone with the right equipment as soon as you call. To do this, they need to know the place and nature of the problem. You can give them your name afterwards.

VICTIM'S AID

Sometimes talking to someone who understands what you've been through can make all the difference between recovering quickly from a serious crime and sinking into despair. For this reason, victims' hot lines have been set up in many places across the country.

If you have suffered as the result of a crime—even if the incident didn't involve you directly—you may benefit greatly from calling one of these hot lines. To find them:

1. Call your local police department or a women's

self-help organization. They're in your phone book.

2. Turn to the blue pages of the phone book. You will find several hot lines—such as *arson hot line, child abuse hot line, narcotics information hot line*—listed on the first page of the Blue Pages under "Easy Reference List—Government Offices."

3. For help after rape, call a local rape hot line. A number of them are listed in the Appendix. This applies both to victims of rape *and* their loved ones. Or call one of the sources of help given in Chapter 15.

4. Contact a victim's-aid organization. These include:

VALOR
Suite 4, F&M Building
210 Laskin Road
Virginia Beach, VA 23541
(804) 422-2692
VALOR provides help to victims of crime.

Victims for Victims
1800 South Robertson Blvd.
Building 6, Suite 400
Los Angeles, CA 90035
(213) 278-4700
Victims for Victims offers victims counseling and sometimes financial aid. It also presses for legislative reforms.

Working Women's Institute
593 Park Avenue
New York, NY 10021
(212)838-4420

Working Women's Institute runs workshops on coping techniques and legal options for women faced with sexual harrassment.

PSYCHOLOGICAL HELP

Talking with good, caring people always helps, but sometimes, just talking with a friend is not enough. Relentless feelings of fear, guilt, and helplessness may continue to trouble you, despite the comfort and reassurance of friends. If this happens, it is wise to seek psychological help.

Here are some guidelines to help you decide if you need a counselor and how to choose one.

1. Look at yourself objectively. Are you having trouble resolving certain feelings? Or do you really just want another shoulder to cry on? If sympathy is all you need, save your money and talk a little more with a friend. It will also help if you make yourself do things that are good for you—exercise, get fresh air daily, give yourself a treat you've been resisting. Chances are you probably just need a little more time to lick your wounds.

2. Try to define your difficulty. This will help you decide whether you need a counselor. If you discover, for instance, that your major trouble is anger at your husband for not showing enough sympathy, your best course may be to tell him about it. But if you find that you are wrestling with feelings and reactions that you can't put to rest, you may benefit from professional care.

If you go to a counselor, you should know what has sent you there. Are you afraid to go out alone? Do you feel guilty that you "let it (the crime) happen?" Even when you know that a feeling is unreasonable, it may still persist. These are the wounds you want the counselor to help you heal. He or she may even help you uncover problems that you didn't realize were there—but you still want help with the feelings you know are bothering you. You should make that clear from the start.

3. To find a counselor: Call a victim's-aid group, your church or synagogue, your doctor, and your

friends. The hot lines and victim's-aid groups mentioned above will usually recommend a counselor skilled in the area where you need help. Many churches and synagogues also have excellent counseling services, usually on a sliding scale. Your doctor may be able to recommend a trustworthy professional. And don't forget your friends! A good counselor has certain personal qualities that only a client can describe. If someone you like found a therapist helpful, chances are you will, too.

YOUR LEGAL RIGHTS

If you have been the victim of a crime, there are three legal entities you should be aware of: crimes, civil wrongs, and victim compensation.

1. A crime is an act committed against the state and prosecuted by the state. Most violent acts are considered crimes. The state prosecutes the assailant through the district attorney, using public funds. The victim does not need to hire a lawyer in order to see the offender brought to trial. She appears only as a witness for the prosecution. The trial won't cost her anything (financially, at least!), but neither will it award her damages should the defendant be found guilty.

The only cost to a victim of a criminal case is a certain amount of time and emotional energy. But the only possible reward is a sense of justice.

To start criminal proceedings, you must file a crime report with the police. If the suspect is arrested, you may be called in to identify him in a line-up. After sifting through the evidence, the prosecutor decides whether it shows the suspect as "guilty beyond a reasonable doubt." If so, there will be a pretrial hearing followed by a court case. You will probably be called as a witness for the prosecution.

2. A civil wrong is an act committed against an individual, prosecuted by the individual at his/her expense. Violent acts can also be considered civil wrongs. Obviously, if someone has injured you personally, he has committed a wrong against you. Therefore, you can prosecute him in civil court as well.

The benefit of a civil suit is obvious: If you win, you may be awarded damages. But there are problems.

To prosecute an assailant in civil court, you must institute proceedings yourself, hire a lawyer, and sometimes pay court costs. This can run into a lot of money. Furthermore, to bring a civil case to court, you must identify and produce the assailant. It's not enough just to know who he is. Usually, the assailant must already have been convicted in criminal court.

And finally, even if you win the case and are awarded damages—you may never see a cent because most offenders simply don't have the cash to pay the damages. Most prison inmates are impoverished and if the criminal court requires them to pay fines, those come first. After the fines and a stint in jail, the criminal usually has nothing left to pay the victim any damages she may have won in court. But she still has to pay her legal fees. Outrageous, yes—but true.

Should you ever consider filing a civil suit against an assailant? Crime experts say yes, but only if you're positive that: (a) your assailant has been convicted in criminal court (that ensures that you will be able to identify and produce him in civil court) and (b) the assailant has enough money to pay you damages.

To find a lawyer: Ask a friend for a recommendation, contact your local lawyer-reference service, or look in the reference section of the *Martindale-Hubbell Law Directory.*

Before we leave civil suits, there is another possibility of which you should be aware. You can sue a person or a company for negligence if you were assaulted in a place with unsafe conditions—such as an apartment house or hotel with faulty locks on the doors or an indoor parking lot with no patrolling guards. Unlike the criminal, these defendants will have the money to pay damages—but also to pay a very good lawyer. Ask your lawyer if you have a good chance before you undertake such a suit.

3. Victim Compensation. Many states now have victim compensation programs, and there are more springing up all the time. Under these programs, the state reimburses the victim for losses suffered through crime. Payments usually cover medical costs and loss of earnings, although a few states also award compensation for pain and suffering. The amount of compensation and qualifications necessary to receive it differ from state to state.

In order to receive compensation, you must report the crime to the police. Then, ask your local police department or your district attorney's office if your state has a compensation program. If it does, describe exactly what happened to you and ask how you qualify and what you should do to receive compensation.

State victim compensation programs are woefully underused. For instance, in New York, only two out of ten eligible victims ever file compensation claims. Yet this is one way you may receive damages for your pains without going to court. Use it!

For more information on victim compensation, contact:

> The National Organization for
> Victim Assistance (NOVA)
> 1757 Park Road N.W.
> Washington, DC 20010
> (202) 232-8560

Of course you should also ask your insurance agent if your losses are covered. Many homeowner's policies cover loss by theft, in or out of the house. Check to see.

SAFETY CHECKS

To Get the Police or Fire Department Quickly

- Write their numbers on every phone in the house and memorize them.

- Locate your neighbor's phone.

- Locate the nearest public phone.

- Remember you can call the operator to reach the police or fire department in an emergency.

- Let the police or fire department know *where* you are and *what's happening* first.

To Get Victim's Aid

- Ask the police or women's groups for hot lines.

- Check the first page of the Blue Pages.

- For rape, call a hot line listed in the Appendix or call an agency listed in chapter 15.

- Contact *VALOR, Victims for Victims,* or *The Working Women's Institute.*

If You're Considering Psychological Help

- Look at yourself objectively and define your problems.

- Contact a victim's-aid group, your place of worship,

- Contact a victim's-aid group, your place of worship, your doctor, or your friends.

Your Legal Rights

- The criminal can be prosecuted in criminal court by the state—with no cost or reward to you.

- He can be prosecuted in civil court at your expense; damages may be awarded to you.

- You may be eligible for victim compensation; ask your police department or district attorney.

APPENDIX

I

BASIC FIRST AID

These are quick, sometimes lifesaving, measures you can take to manage a potentially serious condition until the doctor arrives—or until you can get to the emergency room. For every case mentioned here, you must call a doctor. The only exception is a successful application of the "Heimlich Maneuver," when the condition is cured by dislodging the food.

TO STOP BLEEDING

1. Press a clean cloth firmly onto the wound.

2. If the bleeding doesn't stop, tie a handkerchief between the wound and the heart.

3. Tighten the knot of the handkerchief until the flow stops. A stick stuck through the knot helps regulate the pressure.

4. Call a doctor.

5. Every fifteen minutes, loosen the knot.

TO RESTORE BREATHING

1. Tilt the head back and pull the jaw open.

2. Pinch the nose closed as you cover the patient's mouth with yours and blow hard into his lungs.

3. Wait about three seconds and repeat.

4. Continue until patient starts breathing.

5. Call a doctor.

TO TREAT BURNS

1. For severe burns from flame, cover with several layers of moist dressings. Don't use ice water or ice. Blot area dry with a clean cloth and loosely apply a dry cloth as a protective covering.

2. For chemical burns, first douse with cold water from tap, then cover with a dressing.

3. In both cases, treat for shock.

4. Call a doctor.

TO TREAT FOR SHOCK
(Unconsciousness, chill, pallor, shallow breathing)

1. Cover the body lightly.

2. Raise the feet.

3. Rub wrists and ankles.

4. Call a doctor.

TO TREAT FOR POISONING

1. First give the patient lots of water to dilute the poison.

2. Then immediately call the nearest poison-control center for advice.

3. If you're told to induce vomiting, give one tablespoon of syrup of ipecac and a glass of water. If not, go straight to the emergency room.

TO STOP CHOKING
(The "Heimlich Maneuver")

1. Stand behind the patient and wrap your arms around his waist.

2. Make a fist and press your thumb against his abdomen —above the navel and below the ribs.

3. Hold your fist with your other hand and push it *in* and *up*. Repeat until the food is dislodged.

IN THE MEDICINE CABINET, KEEP:

- Sterile gauze dressings
- Adhesive tape
- Syrup of ipecac
- Tweezers
- Rolls of gauze bandage
- Calamine lotion
- Band-Aids
- Thermometer

BY EVERY PHONE, KEEP THE NUMBERS OF:

- Police
- Fire department
- Ambulance service
- Doctors
- Poison-control center
- Closest 24-hour pharmacy

II
HOW TO AVOID BEING CONNED

Con artists abound. They thrive on four human frailties: *ignorance, fear, greed,* and *grief.* In other words, they con you when your common sense is asleep. Take these precautions—and you won't be "taken":

1. If grief, greed, or fear pushes you to say "Yes" to something—say "No."

2. If you don't know a product well, buy it from an established, reputable dealer.

3. Never give money to a stranger except as an act of charity.

4. Don't believe any get-rich-quick promises.

5. Don't enroll in schools that guarantee you'll find a job after completing the course.

6. Don't send money through the mail for work-at-home money-making schemes.

7. Don't let a police officer or FBI agent in your house until you've called for verification of his name and number.

8. Don't help anyone with a criminal investigation. The police use their own personnel, not private citizens.

9. Don't pay for anything ordered by someone who recently died; you are not obligated to do so.

10. Heed the warning of the Better Business Bureau: "If something sounds too good to be true, it probably is."

III
INSURANCE–
WHAT YOU DO
AND DON'T NEED

There are two types of insurance: mandatory and voluntary. Mandatory insurance includes:

- Fire insurance for a house with a mortgage
- Liability insurance for a car in financial responsibility states
- Collision insurance on a car being financed

Since you have no choice about taking out mandatory insurance, we won't discuss it here. Instead, we'll take a closer look at three basic types of voluntary insurance: life, health, and home.

First, three general guidelines:

1. Insurance is for catastrophes, not mishaps. Take high deductibles at lower premiums.

2. To pay less, pay by the year, not half year.

3. If you (a) are single, (b) rent, (c) don't drive, (d) work at a regular job—you probably have enough insurance already.

LIFE INSURANCE

1. You need it if someone depends on you for survival.

2. A *term policy* pays benefits if you die within a specified period. Experts say term is the best, as it offers good protection at the lowest cost. Although it has no cash value, its premiums are the lowest. A convertible, guaranteed-renewable policy will meet changing needs.

3. A *straight life policy* offers protection for life and is noncancellable for reasons of health. It does have cash value, but this is low compared to other investments. For the same yearly premium, term gives you more insurance protection.

4. Government-controlled programs or large group policies cost less. Some are: Savings Bank Insurance in New York, Connecticut, and Massachusetts; State Life Insurance Fund of Wisconsin; Teachers' Insurance and Annuity Association; College Retirement Equities Fund; Presbyterian Ministers' Fund; Church Life Insurance Corporation.

HEALTH INSURANCE

1. You want insurance that covers *major* illnesses, hospitalization, and medical expenses.

2. Get a noncancellable, guaranteed-renewable policy.

3. Women often have trouble getting private coverage. It helps to join a professional group that offers group health insurance. You are more likely to get coverage, and at cheaper rates.

4. Disability insurance is not always worth its cost. It's expensive and its coverage is very limited. Also, if you are disabled, you may be eligible for social security, workman's compensation, state disability funds, or disability coverage on your life insurance policy.

HOME INSURANCE

1. Buy a homeowner's policy through a good independent casualty agent who will shop around to meet your needs.

2. A *homeowner's policy* is a package that insures your house and possessions against loss by fire, nature, and theft. It also protects you against personal liability for injuries to others on your property. The homeowner's policy will cost you 20 percent less than you would pay for those policies separately, and its fire coverage is usually better than a regular fire insurance policy.

3. If you want the additional coverage that is usually required for valuables (furs, costly jewelry, etc.), ask your agent to outline the appropriate rider for you. Read it carefully to see just what it covers.

4. *Federal crime insurance* offers further coverage against crime. Some states offer insurance, too. Ask your agent.

IV
WEAPONS

Should you arm yourself for self-defense? Here's what crime experts have found about the various weapons used.

GUNS
These are the facts:

1. All studies show that owning a gun increases your chances of injury.

2. If you own a gun, it is more likely that you will be shot by the criminal than that you will shoot him. Shooting to kill someone will not come naturally to you. If you hesitate for a second, the criminal can grab your gun and use it to kill you.

Over half the police officers who die by gunfire are killed with their own guns. You can imagine what that implies for an untrained civilian.

3. If you own a gun, you are four times more likely to be killed by a relative in an argument than by a criminal during a burglary or robbery.

4. If you own a gun, you are six times more likely to accidentally kill yourself or a member of your family than you are to die by criminal attack.

Now decide whether a gun is good protection or not.

TEAR GAS
A canister of tear gas can serve you well if it's ready in your hand and if it's working. You must test these canisters regularly. A blast of tear gas in the face will shock most offend-

ers and vicious animals into momentary paralysis. But it can also spur a criminal to shoot. As always, you must use your common sense. Also, find out if tear gas is legal in your state. It may seem absurd that the victim could end up on trial for breaking the law—but it's happened.

EVERYDAY OBJECTS

One of the dangers of guns is that they are obvious weapons that put the criminal on the alert and help gird him for attack. Although they can be lethal, everyday objects don't look like weapons, thus you can use them before the criminal notices them. Some very effective objects-turned-weapons are:

- A sharp pencil held tightly in your fist. Clench the pencil in your fist, with the point sticking between your fingers and the other end against your palm. Stab it into the eyes, throat, or groin.

- Hard objects, such as a cane, a stick, a book, a solid pocketbook, a briefcase, a rock. Smash them on vital areas, using quick, sharp hits.

- Keys. Holding them in your fist, rake them across the attacker's face.

- A chair. Hold it in front of you with the legs facing out and the back parallel to the floor. Thrust it as hard as you can against the criminal's throat or groin. If he tugs at it, pull back twice, then let loose and shove forward against him.

V

RAPE HOT LINES ACROSS THE NATION

Here is a partial list of rape hot lines taken from the NCPCR (National Center for the Prevention and Control of Rape) *1980 National Directory of Rape Prevention and Treatment Resources.* *

Alabama	Rape Response Program	205-323-7273
Alaska	Standing Together Against Rape	907-276-7273
Arizona	Center Against Sexual Assault	602-257-8095
Arkansas	Rape Crisis, Inc.	501-375-5181
California	Bay Area Women Against Rape	415-845-7273
Colorado	Sexual Assault Task Force	303-925-5400
Connecticut	YMCA Sexual Assault Crisis Service	203-522-6666
Delaware	Rape Crisis Center of Wilmington	302-658-5011
Florida	Rape Treatment Center, Miami	305-325-6949
Georgia	Rape Crisis Center, Atlanta	404-588-4861
Idaho	Rape Crisis Alliance	208-345-7273
Illinois	Women in Crisis Can Act, Inc.	312-929-5150
Indiana	Crisis Intervention Service	317-353-5947
Iowa	Sexual Assault Care Center	515-292-1101
Kansas	Rape Victim Support Service, Inc.	913-841-2345

---

*To receive a copy of the directory, write to:
    The National Center for the Prevention and Control of Rape
    National Institute of Mental Health
    5600 Fishers Lane
    Rockville, MD 20857
    (301) 443-1910

Louisiana	HELPLINE	318-445-4357
Maine	Rape Crisis Center, Greater Portland	207-774-3613
Maryland	Center for Victims of Sexual Assault	301-656-9449
Massachusetts	Rape Crisis Intervention Program	617-735-3337
Michigan	Assault Crisis Center	313-994-1616
Minnesota	Aid to Victims of Sexual Assault	800-232-1300
Missouri	Rape Crisis Assistance, Inc.	417-866-1969
Montana	Billings Rape Task Force	406-259-6506
Nebraska	Rape/Spouse Abuse Crisis Center	402-475-7273
Nevada	Community Action Against Rape	702-735-7111
New Hampshire	Women's Crisis Line	603-668-2299
New Jersey	Sexual Assault Rape Analysis Unit	201-733-7273
New Mexico	Santa Fe Rape Crisis Center, Inc.	505-982-4667
New York	Rape Intervention Program	212-870-1875
North Carolina	Chapel Hill–Carrboro Rape Crisis	919-967-7273
North Dakota	Rape & Abuse Center	701-293-7273
Ohio	Akron Rape Crisis Center	216-434-7273
Oklahoma	Rape Crisis	405-524-7273
Oregon	Rape Crisis Center	503-754-0110
Pennsylvania	Women Organized Against Rape	215-922-3434
Puerto Rico	Centro de Ayuda	809-765-2285
South Carolina	People Against Rape	803-722-7273
South Dakota	R.E.A.C.T.	605-688-4518
Tennessee	Knoxville Rape Crisis Center	615-522-7273
Utah	YWCA Women's Crisis Shelter	801-392-7273
Vermont	Women's Rape Crisis Center	802-863-1236
Virginia	Charlottesville Rape Crisis Center	804-977-7273
Washington	Seattle Rape Relief	206-632-7273
West Virginia	Sexual Assault Information Center	304-344-9834
Wisconsin	Green Bay Rape Crisis Center, Ltd.	414-433-0584
Wyoming	Western Wyoming Mental Health Association	800-442-6383